Licens SOUTH CAROLINA 2016

Concealed Weapon Permit Handbook

by Elbert T. (Ted) Landreth, Jr.

SLED/NRA Certified Instructor

ISBN: 978-1-329-86489-4

Shooterszone Tactical
Greenville, South Carolina
www.shooterszone.com

Printed and bound in the United States of America

Disclaimer

This publication is designed to provide the reader with accurate and authoritative information in regard to the subject matter covered. It is sold with the explicit understanding that the writer or publisher is not engaged in the business of rendering professional legal services. If legal advice or other expert assistance is required, the services of a competent professional should be sought. Neither the author nor publisher assumes any responsibility for the use or misuse of any information contained in this publication.

"A free people ought not only to be armed and disciplined, but they should have sufficient arms and ammunition to maintain a status of independence from any who might attempt to abuse them, which would include their own government."

- George Washington

Introduction

Licensed to Carry - South Carolina - Concealed Weapon Permit Handbook was originally created as a training manual for South Carolina Concealed Weapon Permit applicants and a reference guide to persons already licensed or permitted.

However, soon after firearm instructors and gun stores became aware of the publication it began selling as a firearm education and safety course for new gun owners as well.

It's like anything, *if you don't use it - you lose it*, and that especially applies to the knowledge of the laws pertaining to the "legal" concealed carry of a handgun.

The laws relating to the concealed carry of a weapon appear complex and very difficult to understand and many times even harder to remember. Questions as to when and where you can lawfully carry your weapon can often become overwhelming, and if you are not thoroughly familiar with applicable laws and regulations, you may find yourself in the middle of a "big and very expensive legal battle."

When in doubt about the laws and regulations that govern your right to carry a concealed weapon, safe handling procedures, or shooting fundamentals, this book will provide you with that much needed information, thereby strengthening the knowledge of what is expected and required of you as a responsible gun owner and a legally armed citizen.

"That right of the people to keep and bear arms shall not be infringed; a well-armed and well-regulated militia being the best security of a free country; but no person religiously scrupulous of bearing arms shall be compelled to render military service in person."

CONTENTS

Chapter 1

Guns & South Carolina Law

- OFFENSES INVOLVING WEAPONS
- REGULATION OF PISTOLS
- CONCEALED WEAPON PERMITS

SOUTH CAROLINA LAWS & FIREARMS -

South Carolina has never been an unreasonably restrictive state in regards to firearms, especially when compared to California, New York, Illinois and a few others which attempt to prohibit private firearm ownership. In those states, gun owners are licensed and the licenses are virtually impossible to acquire. Due to numerous legal exceptions provided by South Carolina law, residents and even visitors to this state have for the most part, felt relatively at ease in the ownership and possession of firearms, including handguns.

In addition to the legal exceptions provided by law for the military, law enforcement, gun dealers and gun repair shops, private citizens can lawfully carry handguns on or about their person, even without a carry permit, provided they are licensed hunters or fishermen on the way to or from such sporting activities, however some restrictions do apply.

Individuals are allowed by law to carry firearms to and from target shooting, on their own private property and can keep them in their homes. Loaded firearms can even be transported in motor vehicles, provided they are stored in closed glove compartments, closed consoles or in the vehicle trunk.

OFFENSES and DEFINATIONS - HANDGUN –

South Carolina law defines a "pistol" as any firearm designed to expel a projectile and designed to be fired from the hand, but not include any firearm recognized or classified as an antique or collector's item, or any that does not fire fixed cartridges. (SECTION 16-23-10)

A *"crime of violence"* means murder, manslaughter (except negligent manslaughter arising out of traffic accidents), rape, mayhem, kidnapping, burglary, robbery, housebreaking, assault with an intent to kill, commit rape, or rob, assault with a dangerous weapon, or assault with an intent to commit any offense punishable by imprisonment for one year or more.

A "*fugitive from justice*" means any person who has fled from or is fleeing from any law enforcement officer to avoid prosecution or imprisonment for a crime of violence.

The term "*subversive organization*" means any group, committee, club, league, society, which purpose is the establish, control, conduct, seize or overthrow the government of the United States or any state or political subdivision thereof, by the use of force, violence, espionage, sabotage, or threats or attempts of any of the foregoing.

The term "*conviction*" is to include pleas of guilty, pleas of nolo contendere and forfeiture of bail.

The term "*Division*" shall mean the State Law Enforcement Division. The terms "purchase" or "sell" mean to knowingly buy, offer to buy,

The term "*person*" shall mean any individual, corporation, company, association, firm, partnership, society or joint stock company.

UNLAWFUL CARRYING OF A FIREARM - EXCEPTIONS

South Carolina law states that it is unlawful for anyone to carry about the person any pistol, whether concealed or not, except under the following circumstances: (SECTION 16-23-20)

(1) regular, salaried law enforcement officers, and reserve police officers of a state agency, municipality, or county of the State, uncompensated Governor's constables, law enforcement officers of the federal government or other states when they are carrying out official duties while in this State, deputy enforcement officers of the Natural Resources Enforcement Division of the Department of Natural Resources, and retired commissioned law enforcement officers employed as private detectives or private investigators;

(2) members of the Armed Forces of the United States, the National Guard, organized reserves, or the State Militia when on duty;

(3) members, or their invited guests, of organizations authorized by law to purchase or receive firearms from the United States or this State or regularly enrolled members, or their invited guests, of

clubs organized for the purpose of target shooting or collecting modern and antique firearms while these members, or their invited guests, are at or going to or from their places of target practice or their shows and exhibits;

(4) licensed hunters or fishermen who are engaged in hunting or fishing or going to or from their places of hunting or fishing while in a vehicle or on foot;

(5) a person regularly engaged in the business of manufacturing, repairing, repossessing, or dealing in firearms, or the agent or representative of this person, while possessing, using, or carrying a handgun in the usual or ordinary course of the business;

(6) guards authorized by law to possess handguns and engaged in protection of property of the United States or any agency of the United States;

(7) members of authorized military or civil organizations while parading or when going to and from the places of meeting of their respective organizations;

(8) a person in his home or upon his real property or a person who has the permission of the owner or the person in legal possession or the person in legal control of the home or real property;

(9) a person in a vehicle if the handgun is:

(a) secured in a closed glove compartment, closed console, closed trunk, or in a closed container secured by an integral fastener and transported in the luggage compartment of the vehicle; however, this item is not violated if the glove compartment, console, or trunk is opened in the presence of a law enforcement officer for the sole purpose of retrieving a driver's license, registration, or proof of insurance. If the person has a valid concealed weapon permit pursuant to Article 4, Chapter 31, Title 23, then the person also may secure his weapon *under a seat in a vehicle, or in any open or closed storage compartment* within the vehicle's passenger compartment; or concealed on or about his person.

(10) a person carrying a handgun unloaded and in a secure wrapper from the place of purchase to his home or fixed place of business or while in the process of changing or moving one's residence or changing or moving one's fixed place of business;

(11) a prison guard while engaged in his official duties;

(12) a person who is granted a permit under provision of law by the State Law Enforcement Division to carry a handgun about his person, under conditions set forth in the permit, and while transferring the handgun between the permittee's person and a location specified in item (9);

(13) the owner or the person in legal possession or the person in legal control of a fixed place of business, while at the fixed place of business, and the employee of a fixed place of business, other than a business subject to Section 16-23-465, while at the place of business; however, the employee may exercise this privilege only after: (a) acquiring a permit pursuant to item (12), and (b) obtaining the permission of the owner or person in legal control or legal possession of the premises;

(14) a person engaged in firearms-related activities while on the premises of a fixed place of business which conducts, as a regular course of its business, activities related to sale, repair, pawn, firearms training, or use of firearms, unless the premises is posted with a sign limiting possession of firearms to holders of permits issued pursuant to item (12);

(15) a person while transferring a handgun directly from or to a vehicle and a location specified in this section where one may legally possess the handgun.

(16) Any person on a motorcycle when the pistol is secured in a closed saddlebag or other similar closed accessory container attached, whether permanently or temporarily to the motorcycle.

SALE OR DELIVERY OF FIREARMS (SECTION 16-23-30)

(A) It is unlawful for a person to knowingly sell, offer to sell, deliver, lease, rent, barter, exchange, or transport for sale into this State any handgun to:

(1) a person who has been convicted of a crime of violence in any court of the United States, the several states, commonwealths, territories, possessions, or the District of Columbia or who is a fugitive from justice or a habitual drunkard or a drug addict or who has been adjudicated mentally incompetent;

(2) a person who is a member of a subversive organization;

(3) a person under the age of eighteen, but this shall not apply to the issue of handguns to members of the Armed Forces of the United States, active or reserve, National Guard, State Militia, or R. O. T. C., when on duty or training or the temporary loan of handguns for instructions under the immediate supervision of a parent or adult instructor; or

(4) a person who by order of a circuit judge or county court judge of this State has been adjudged unfit to carry or possess a firearm, such adjudication to be made upon application by any police officer, or by any prosecuting officer of this State, or sua sponte, by the court, but a person who is the subject of such an application is entitled to reasonable notice and a proper hearing prior to any such adjudication.

(B) It is unlawful for a person enumerated in subsection (A) to possess or acquire handguns within this State.

(C) A person shall not knowingly buy, sell, transport, pawn, receive, or possess any stolen handgun or one from which the original serial number has been removed or obliterated.

POINTING A FIREARM AT ANY PERSON -

South Carolina law states that it is unlawful for a person to present or point a loaded or unloaded firearm at another person. A person in violation of this law is guilty of a felony and, upon conviction, must be fined in the discretion of the court or imprisoned not more than five years. This rule of law should not to be construed as such to prevent a person's right of self-defense or to apply to theatrical performances. (SECTION 16-23-410)

The law clearly defines that you cannot point a firearm at another person_unless you are acting legally to defend yourself, others, your home or property. The law does not allow you to point a firearm, loaded or unloaded at another person without due cause.

GUNS IN THE WORKPLACE

Employers, public and private may choose to prohibit employees from carrying a weapon while on the premises of the business or work place, or while using any machinery, vehicle, or equipment owned or operated by the business. South Carolina law expressly upholds the right of employers to prohibit persons permitted to carry a concealed weapon from carrying a weapon on the employer's premises, if the employer chooses to do so. (SECTION 23-31-220)

The posting of a sign stating *"No Concealable Weapons Allowed"* by the employer, owner, or person in legal possession or control of the business shall constitute sufficient notice to a person holding a concealed weapons permit issued pursuant to South Carolina law that the employer, owner, or person in legal possession or control requests that concealable weapons are not be brought upon the premises or into the work place.

Any person who, without legal cause or good excuse, enters into the place of business or work place after having been warned not to do so or any person who, having entered into the place of business, without having been warned fails and refuses, without good cause or good excuse, to leave immediately upon being requested to do so by the employer, owner, or person in legal possession or control, on conviction, be fined not more than two hundred dollars or be imprisoned for not more than thirty days. In addition to the penalties above, a person convicted of a second or subsequent violation of the provisions of this paragraph must have his permit revoked for a period of one year. (Section 16-11-620)

REQUIRED PERMISSION ON PRIVATE PROPERTY

Property owners or those in lawful possession of the property (tenants of rented property) may control whether persons coming onto that property are allowed to carry concealed weapons, even with a lawfully-issued permit. Expressed permission is required to carry a concealable weapon into a private residence.

Any person who, without legal cause or good excuse, enters into the residence of another person after having been warned not to do so or any person who, having entered into the residence or on the premises of another person without having been warned fails and refuses, without good cause or good excuse to immediately leave upon being ordered or requested to do so by the person in possession or his agent or representative can, on conviction, be fined up to two hundred dollars or be jailed up to thirty days. (SECTION 23-31-225)

HOTELS – MOTELS and FIREARMS - (SECTION 23-31-230)

In South Carolina, any person who is legally allowed to possess a firearm may carry a concealable weapon from an automobile or other motorized means of transportation to a room or other accommodation he has rented and upon which an accommodation's tax has been paid.

SIGN EQUIREMENTS (SECTION 23-31-235)

SECTION 5. Section 23-31-235 of the 1976 Code, as added by Act 464 of 1996, is amended to read:

Section 23-31-235 - (A) Notwithstanding any other provision of this article, any requirement of or allowance for the posting of signs prohibiting the carrying of a concealable weapon upon any premises shall only be satisfied by a sign expressing the prohibition in both written language interdict and universal sign language.

(B) All signs must be posted at each entrance into a building where a concealable weapon permit holder is prohibited from carrying a concealable weapon and must be:

(1) clearly visible from outside the building;

(2) eight inches wide by twelve inches tall in size;

(3) contain the words 'NO CONCEALABLE WEAPONS ALLOWED' in black one-inch tall uppercase type at the bottom of the sign and centered between the lateral edges of the sign;

(4) contain a black silhouette of a handgun inside a circle seven inches in diameter with a diagonal line that runs from the lower left to the upper right at a forty-five degree angle from the horizontal;

(5) a diameter of a circle; and

(6) placed not less than forty inches and not more than sixty inches from the bottom of the building's entrance door.

(C) If the premises where concealable weapons are prohibited does not have doors, then the signs contained in subsection (A) must be:

(1) thirty-six inches wide by forty-eight inches tall in size;

(2) contain the words 'NO CONCEALABLE WEAPONS ALLOWED' in black three-inch tall uppercase type at the bottom of the sign and centered between the lateral edges of the sign;

(3) contain a black silhouette of a handgun inside a circle thirty-four inches in diameter with a diagonal line that is two inches wide and runs from the lower left to the upper right at a forty-five degree angle from the horizontal and must be a diameter of a circle whose circumference is two inches wide;

(4) placed not less than forty inches and not more than ninety-six inches above the ground;

(5) posted in sufficient quantities to be clearly visible from any point of entry onto the premises.

Persons allowed to carry a concealed weapon while on duty (SECTION 23-31-240)

The following persons who possess a valid permit pursuant to this article may carry a concealable weapon anywhere within this State, when carrying out the duties of their office:

(1) active Supreme Court justices;
(2) active judges of the court of appeals;
(3) active circuit court judges;
(4) active family court judges;
(5) active masters-in-equity;
(6) active probate court judges;
(7) active magistrates;
(8) active municipal court judges;
(9) active federal judges;
(10) active administrative law judges;
(11) active solicitors and assistant solicitors; and
(12) active workers' compensation commissioners.

DRUG & ALCOHOL TESTING FOLLOWING A SHOOTING -

If a law enforcement officer has probable cause to believe that a person used a firearm while under the influence of alcohol or a controlled substance and caused the death or serious bodily injury of an individual, the person shall submit at the request of the officer, to a blood-alcohol test to determine the alcohol level or for the presence of a controlled substance. (SECTION 23-31-415)

If the arresting officer does not request a breath or urine test of the person arrested for an offense allegedly committed while the person was using a firearm while under the influence of alcohol or a controlled substance, the person may request the arresting officer to have a breath test made to determine the alcohol content of the person's blood or a urine test for the purpose of determining the presence of a controlled substance.

The failure of the person who requests a breath or urine test to actually be tested shall bar the prosecution of the person for using a firearm while under the influence of alcohol or a controlled substance.

A criminal charge resulting from an incident causing the officer's demand for testing should be tried in addition to the charge of *using a firearm while under the influence of alcohol or a controlled substance*. (SECTION 23-31-400)

If the charges are tried separately, the fact that the person refused, resisted, obstructed, or opposed testing is admissible at the trial of the criminal offense which precipitated the demand for testing. The results of any test administered pursuant to this section for the purpose of detecting the presence of a controlled substance is not admissible as evidence in a criminal prosecution for the possession of a controlled substance.

The results of a test administered pursuant to this section for the purpose of detecting the presence of a controlled substance are not admissible as evidence in criminal prosecution for the possession of a controlled substance.

Information obtained pursuant to this section must be released to a court, prosecuting attorney, defense attorney, or law enforcement officer in connection with an alleged violation of Section 23-31-400 upon request for this information.

PRESUMPTIONS

Upon the trial of a civil or criminal action or proceeding arising out of acts alleged to have been committed by a person while using a firearm while under the influence of alcohol or a controlled substance, the results of any test administered pursuant to Section 23-1-410 or 23-31-415 and this section are admissible into evidence, and the amount of alcohol in the person's blood at the time alleged, as shown by chemical analysis of the person's blood or breath, creates lawful presumptions under law. (SECTION 23-31-420 (1)(2)(3))

South Carolina law states that it is <u>unlawful for anyone to carry about the person any handgun, whether concealed or not, without exceptions as provided by law</u>. A person violating the law is guilty of a misdemeanor and upon conviction, may be fined up to a thousand dollars or imprisoned up to a one year, or both. (*About the person is defined as <u>being readily accessible or convenient for immediate use</u> even if the gun is not physically touching the person's body*).

SOUTH CAROLINA CONCEALED WEAPON PERMIT

By taking and successfully completing a *South Carolina Concealed Weapon Permit Training Course* and obtaining a permit, you can substantially broaden your freedom to carry a handgun.

There are politicians on all levels and antigun activist that strongly oppose our gun freedoms, and detest the fact that private citizens possess firearms, much less the fact that private citizens can be issued concealed weapon permits. These gun freedom opponents' are very powerful and are constantly looking for people who have received concealed carry permits, and in one way or another violate the law, whether intentionally or through carelessness or ignorance.

They use indiscretions of the law to fuel their lobbying efforts for the passing of antigun laws, and more attempts to overturn the laws that provide you and me the freedom to obtain a permit, and the right to carry a concealed weapon. For that reason, it is crucial that every permit holder act above reproach in the manner in which he or she conducts them self, especially when carrying a firearm.

KEEP YOUR PERMIT IN YOUR IMMEDIATE POSSESSION

The law requires that anyone who is carrying a handgun by virtue of a concealed carry permit, have the permit in his/her possession any time he/she is carrying a handgun. South Carolina code SECTION 23-31-215-K as amended (2002), states, "*<u>A permit holder must have his permit identification card in his possession whenever he carries a concealable weapon</u>*."

Furthermore, if you have a concealed carry permit and you are carrying a handgun pursuant to South Carolina's *Law Abiding Citizens Self-Defense Act of 1996* (SECTION 23-31-215-K) the law requires that you immediately inform a law enforcement officer of the fact that you are a permit holder and present your permit identification card when an officer (1) identifies himself as a law enforcement officer and (2) requests identification or a driver's license from you.

Hypothetically, let's imagine that you are pulled over by a law enforcement officer for a traffic violation, and the officer requests to see your driver's license. In South Carolina and in most states, if you are carrying a concealed handgun on your person, you are required by law to present your concealed weapon permit to the officer, along with your state driver's license.

This means that <u>any time a permit holder is carrying a concealed handgun</u> and he or she is approached by an officer who introduces himself as an officer of the law and request a driver's license or other identification from the permit holder, the permit holder is required by law to produce their permit identification card to the officer. Failure to do so is a criminal violation and is punishable by a fine or jail time.

It's very simple, if you come to a license check, you get pulled over for a speeding violation, or for any other reason whatsoever, if you are carrying a concealed handgun, you must immediately inform the officer that you have a concealed weapons permit and that you are armed.

<u>Inform the officer in that order – don't just announce, "*I have a gun*", without first stating that you have a concealed weapons permit</u>.

Since most shootings of law enforcement officers take place at traffic stops, this requirement is a necessary safety precaution. In today's society, officers generally feel a little anxious when they approach a car he or she has just stopped. The reason being, they don't know what circumstances they may face when they reach the driver and passengers of the vehicle.

For your safety and for the safety of the officer, if you are driving, you must remain seated in the driver's seat. All passengers should remain in their place. <u>Do not get out of the vehicle</u> unless you are instructed to do so by an officer, place both hands on the steering wheel (10 and 2 position) and remain in that position until the officer directs you otherwise.

<u>Do not reach for your wallet or purse</u>; <u>do not attempt to open the glove box</u> for your vehicle ownership or insurance information. <u>Remain still with your hands placed on the steering wheel</u>!

Any unnecessary movement or actions, no matter how innocent, may cause the officer to think that you may be reaching for a gun or other weapon, and the situation could turn tragic. It is recommended that you instruct any adult passengers riding in the vehicle with you to follow the same safety procedures.

If our law enforcement officials conclude that concealed carry laws are creating a significant threat to the safety of our law enforcement personnel, or to the public at large, they too could be compelled to join the lobbying efforts against concealed carry laws.

<u>You must always remain above reproach in the manner in which you conduct yourself in respect to the law</u>.

PERMIT <u>MUST</u> BE IN YOUR IMMEDIATE POSSESSION

REMINDER: It is extremely important that you understand and remember this requirement! (1) A permit holder **must** have his permit identification card in his immediate possession whenever he carries a concealable weapon. (2) A permit holder **must** inform a law enforcement officer of the fact that he is a permit holder and present the permit identification card <u>when</u> an officer (1) identifies himself as a law enforcement officer and (2) requests identification or a driver's license from a permit holder. A person who violates the provisions of this subsection is guilty of a misdemeanor and, upon conviction, must be fined twenty-five dollars. SECTION 23-31-215 (K)

LOST | STOLEN | DAMAGED PERMITS -

SLED shall issue a replacement for lost, stolen, damaged, or destroyed permit identification cards after the permit holder has updated all information required in the original application and the payment of a five-dollar replacement fee. A permit holder immediately must report the loss or theft of a permit identification card to SLED headquarters.

CHANGE OF PERMANENT ADDRESS –

Any change of a permanent address must be communicated in writing to SLED within ten days of the change accompanied by the payment of a fee of five dollars for the cost of issuance of a new permit. SLED will issue a new permit with the updated address.

A permit holder's failure to notify SLED in accordance with this subsection constitutes a misdemeanor punishable by a twenty-five-dollar fine. The original permit shall remain in force until receipt of the corrected permit identification card by the permit holder at which time the original permit must be returned to SLED.

PROHIBITED CARRY LOCATIONS –

A permit issued pursuant to this section does not authorize a permit holder to carry a concealable weapon into a:

(1) police, sheriff, or highway patrol station or any other law enforcement office or facility;

(2) detention facility, prison, or jail or any other correctional facility or office;

(3) courthouse or courtroom;

(4) polling place on election days;

(5) office of or the business meeting of the governing body of a county, public school district, municipality, or special purpose district;

(6) school or college athletic event not related to firearms;

(7) day care facility or pre-school facility;

(8) place where the carrying of firearms is prohibited by federal law;

(9) church or other established religious sanctuary unless express permission is given by the appropriate church official or governing body;

(10) hospital, medical clinic, doctor's office, or any other facility where medical services or procedures are performed, unless expressly authorized by the employer.

A person who willfully violates a provision of this subsection is guilty of a misdemeanor and, upon conviction, must be fined not less than one thousand dollars or imprisoned not more than one year, or both, at the discretion of the court and have his permit revoked for five years.

PERMIT RECIPROCITY & RECOGNITION -

Reciprocity refers to a mutual agreement between two states that agree to honor each other's concealed carry permits. When a state honors another state's concealed carry permit, but the other state does not honor that state's permit, it is called *recognition.* For example, the State of Utah honors South Carolina's permits; however South Carolina does not honor Utah's permits.

Valid out-of-state carry permits held by residents of reciprocal states will be honored in this state. SLED has the authority to decide as to those states which have permit issuance standards equal to or greater than the standards contained in this state. (See Chapter 16, Page – 144 for a complete list of the states with which South Carolina has reciprocity, state recognition or universal recognition, which means a state would treat CCW permits like driver's licenses, allowing current permit holders to carry in the state with any valid permit.)

U.S. POST OFFICES - FIREARMS

Carrying a Firearm on or in US Postal Service Property Conduct on Postal Property - 39 CFR 232.1

(l) Weapons and explosives. <u>No person while on postal property may carry firearms</u>, other dangerous or deadly weapons, or explosives, either openly or concealed, <u>or store the same on postal property</u>, except for official purposes. This section applies to all real property under the charge and control of the Postal Service, to all tenant agencies, and to all persons entering in or on such property.

The question as to the legality in regards to carrying a firearm into Postal Service property has been an issue of much debate. Some groups even insist that our right to *"Keep and Bear Arms"* as provided by the Second Amendment takes precedence over US Code of Federal Regulations "postal firearm ban". Regardless of the many opinions the simple fact remains, it is a violation of federal law *39 C.F.R. § 232.1(l)* and a violation of some states' criminal statutes.

The United States Fifth Circuit Court of Appeals (Eastern District of Louisiana) on October 14, 2009 held that the Second Amendment does not prohibit a Postal Service regulation banning firearms from its facilities. The court's decision confirmed the ruling by lower courts that the US Postal Service is justified in enforcing federal regulation Code 39 C.F.R. § 232.1(l) in taking the position that its <u>firearm ban applies not only to the building and the employee/working parking lots, but to any and all public parking lots located on the post office property</u> where an individual might park a vehicle while checking their mail. This means that the Postal Service can prosecute you for a federal crime even if you leave your firearm in the car while checking your post office box.

In additional to a federal violation, South Carolina Code of Law SECTION 16-23-420 states that carrying or displaying firearms in public buildings or areas adjacent thereto is a felony that carries a prison term not to exceed five (5) years and a fine of no more than $5,000 or both.

RESTAURANTS AND BARS - FIREARMS

South Carolina law allows for a Concealed Weapons Permit (CWP) holder to carry a concealed weapon into an establishment that serves alcoholic liquor, beer or wine for on site consumption, <u>provided that the permittee does not consume alcohol while on the premises if in possession of the weapon</u>. (Section 23-31-215)

A property owner, lease holder or the management of a business may prohibit the carrying of concealable weapons into the business by the posting of a sign stating "**NO CONCEALABLE WEAPONS ALLOWED**". (Section 23-31-235)

A property owner, lease holder or the management of a business may request that a person carrying a concealable weapon leave the business' premises, or any portion of the premises, or request that a person carrying a concealed weapon remove the weapon from the business' premises, or any portion of the premises. (Section 23-31-235)

A person carrying a concealed weapon who refuses to leave a business' premises or portion of the premises after being requested or who refuses to remove the concealed weapon from a business' premises or portion of the premises when requested may be criminally charged with a misdemeanor, and if convicted must be fined not more than two thousand dollars or imprisoned not more than two years, or both.

GUNS IN THE WORKPLACE

Employers, public and private may choose to prohibit employees from carrying a weapon while on the premises of the business or work place, or while using any machinery, vehicle, or equipment owned or operated by the business. South Carolina law expressly upholds the right of employers to prohibit persons permitted to carry a concealed weapon from carrying a weapon on the employer's premises, if the employer chooses to do so. (SECTION 23-31-220)

The posting of a sign stating **"NO CONCEALABLE WEAPONS ALLOWED"** by the employer, owner, or person in legal possession or control of the business shall constitute sufficient notice to a person holding a concealed weapons permit issued pursuant to South Carolina law that the employer, owner, or person in legal possession or control requests that concealable weapons are not to be brought upon the premises or into the work place.

Any person who, without legal cause or good excuse, enters into the place of business or work place after having been warned not to do so or any person who, having entered into the place of business, without having been warned fails and refuses, without good cause or good excuse, to leave immediately upon being requested to do so by the employer, owner, or person in legal possession or control, on conviction, be fined not more than two hundred dollars or be imprisoned for not more than thirty days. (Section 16-11-620)

In addition to the penalties above, a person convicted of a second or subsequent violation of the provisions of this paragraph must have his permit revoked for a period of one year.

PRIVATE PROPERTY - PERMISSION REQUIRED

Property owners or those in lawful possession of the property (tenants of rented property) may control whether persons coming onto that property are allowed to carry concealed weapons, even with a lawfully-issued permit. Expressed permission is required to carry a concealable weapon into a private residence.

Any person who, without legal cause or good excuse, enters into the residence of another person after having been warned not to do so or any person who, having entered into the residence or on the premises of another person without having been warned fails and refuses, without good cause or good excuse, to immediately leave upon being ordered or requested to do so by the person in possession or his agent or representative can, on conviction, be fined up to two hundred dollars or be jailed up to thirty days. (SECTION 23-31-225)

SOUTH CAROLINA STATE PARKS - FIREARMS

Possessing any firearm, air gun, explosive, or firework except by duly authorized park personnel, law enforcement officers, or persons using areas specifically designated by the department for use of firearms, air guns, fireworks, or explosives.

Licensed hunters may have firearms in their possession during hunting seasons provided that such firearms are unloaded and carried in a case or the trunk of a vehicle except that in designated game management areas where hunting is permitted, licensed hunters may use firearms for hunting in the manner authorized by law.

This subsection shall not apply to a person carrying a concealable weapon pursuant to Article 4, Chapter 31, Title 23, and the concealable weapon and its ammunition."

Individuals holding a valid concealed weapon permit issued pursuant to South Carolina Section 23-31-215 are authorized by law to carry a concealed weapon in state parks under the control of the Department of Parks, Recreation, and Tourism. SECTION 51-3-145(G)

SCHOOL PROPERTY – FIREARMS

It is unlawful for a person to possess a firearm of any kind on any premises or property owned, operated, or controlled by a private or public school, college, university, technical college, other post secondary institution, or in any publicly owned building, without the express permission of the authorities in charge of the premises or property.

EXECPTION - A person who possesses a valid concealed weapons permit pursuant to South Carolina's *Law Abiding Citizens Self-Defense Act of 1996* (Article 4, Chapter 31, Title 23) is exempt from this restriction provided that the weapon remains inside an attended or locked motor vehicle and is secured in a closed glove compartment, closed console, closed trunk, or a closed container secured by an integral fastener and transported in the luggage compartment of the vehicle.

It is unlawful for a person to enter the premises or property described above and to display, brandish, or threaten others with a firearm. Any person who violates this law is guilty of a felony and, upon conviction, can be fined up to five thousand dollars or imprisoned up to five years, or both.

A married student residing in an apartment provided by the private or public school whose presence with a weapon in or around a particular building is authorized by persons legally responsible for the security of the buildings is also exempted from this section.

The terms 'premises' and 'property' <u>do not include</u> state or locally owned or maintained roads, streets, or rights-of-way of them, running through or adjacent to premises or property owned, operated, or controlled by a private or public school, college, university, technical college, or other post-secondary institution, which are open full time to public vehicular traffic.

INTERSTATE HIGHWAY REST AREA - FIREARMS

South Carolina law provides that persons with a valid concealed weapons permit from this state or a reciprocal state may lawfully carry a concealed firearm when upon any premises, property, or building that is part of an interstate highway rest area facility.

UNLAWFUL DISCHARGING OF A FIREARM-

It is a violation of state law for a person to discharge or cause to be discharged unlawfully a firearm at or into a residential dwelling, other building, structure, or enclosure normally occupied by persons. A person in violation of this law is guilty of a felony and upon conviction, may be fined up to one-thousand dollars or imprisoned up to ten years, or both.

It is a violation of the law for a person to unlawfully discharge firearms at or into any vehicle, aircraft, water craft, or other conveyance, device, or equipment while it is occupied. A person convicted of violating these provisions may be fined up to one thousand dollars or imprisoned up to ten years, or both.

CONCEALED WEAPONS | FORFEITURE OF WEAPONS

Any person carrying a deadly weapon usually used for the infliction of personal injury concealed about his person is guilty of a misdemeanor, must forfeit to the county, or, if convicted in a municipal court, to the municipality the weapon, and must be fined not less than two hundred dollars nor more than five hundred dollars or imprisoned not less than thirty days nor more than ninety days.

Nothing herein contained may be construed to apply to (1) persons carrying concealed weapons upon their own premises or pursuant to and in compliance with Article 4 of Chapter 31 of Title 23, or (2) peace officers in the actual discharge of their duties. These provisions do not apply to rifles, shotguns, dirks, slingshots, metal knuckles, or razors unless they are used with the intent to commit a crime or in furtherance of a crime.

SIGNS: <u>No Concealed Weapons Allowed!</u>

Notwithstanding any other provision of this article, any requirement of or allowance for the posting of signs prohibiting the carrying of a concealable weapon upon any premises shall only be satisfied by a sign expressing the prohibition in both written language interdict and universal sign language, if you ignore and violate the notice, you may be charged with a criminal trespass, and upon conviction, you may be subject to a fine and/or a thirty day jail term. SECTION 23-31-235(A)

PROHIBITED CARRY – CONVICTIONS – PENALTIES-

Premises of a private or public school, college, university, technical college, other post-secondary institution [without express permission of person in charge of premises][16-23-4201

[Felony - $5000 fine and/or 5-years imprisonment]

Inside publicly-owned building of any kind, except at Interstate 4

[Felony - $5000 fine and/or 5-years imprisonment]

Inside an establishment licensed for on-premises consumption of alcohol premises [116-23-465]

[Misdemeanor - $2000 fine and/or 3-years imprisonment]

Premises of a private residence without permission [23-31-225]

[Misdemeanor - $1000 fine and/or 1-year imprisonment]

Any place where carrying is prohibited by proper sign [23-31-2201

[Violation - $200 fine or 30-days imprisonment]

EXCEPTIONS: Active Justices, Judges, Masters-in-equity, Solicitors, Assistant Solicitors and Workers Compensation Commissioners [23-31-240]

It is important to remember that a concealed weapon permit does not authorize you to use a weapon - it only authorizes you to carry it.

The use of a handgun is regulated by other state laws and it is you responsibility to become familiar with those laws in order to keep from violating them.

Chapter 2

The Concealed Weapon Permit Application

The South Carolina Law Enforcement Division (SLED) is the regulatory agency charged by South Carolina law to enforce South Carolina's concealed weapon permit program. SLED is the official abbreviation for the South Carolina Law Enforcement Division.

"The Law Abiding Citizens Self-Defense Act of 1996"

SOUTH CAROLINA CONCEALED WEAPON PERMIT APPLICATION

Mail completed application form/enclosures to: CWP Application, SLED Regulatory, PO Box 21398, Columbia, SC 29221

Please check if any of the following apply (proper documentation must be submitted as indicated below):

Disabled Veteran:_____ Retired/Former Military:_____ Active Military:_____ Retired Law Enforcement:_____ Active Law Enforcement:_____

Application Type (New/Renewal): _____ CWP # (Renewal Only): _____

Full Name (Last, First, Middle, Maiden, Suffix): _____

Residence Address: _____ Mailing Address: _____

City: _____ State: _____ Zip: _____ County: _____

Social Security #: _____ DL/ID Card #: _____ Alien #: _____

Date of Birth (YYYY/MM/DD): _____ Place of Birth: _____

Race: _____ Sex: _____ Height: _____ Weight: _____ Eye Color: _____ Hair Color: _____

Home Phone: _____ Business Phone: _____ Cell Phone: _____ E-Mail: _____

Training Date: _____ Instructor Cert. #: _____ Student #: _____

Instructor Signature: _____ Date: _____

You must answer the following three questions. If any of the answers are "No" you will not be eligible for a permit.

Are you a South Carolina resident or qualified non-resident (Section 23-31-210, S.C. Code of Laws)? ☐ Yes ☐ No
Have you successfully completed the required training (Section 23-31-210, S.C. Code of Laws)? ☐ Yes ☐ No
Are you allowed by all applicable federal/state laws and court orders to possess a handgun? ☐ Yes ☐ No

---

INSTRUCTIONS- REVIEW CAREFULLY BEFORE APPLICATION SUBMISSION:

For questions about the CWP application process, forms, or if you need information on state laws and regulations, please visit www.sled.sc.gov

- Processing time may be up to 90 days. A renewal application should be mailed 90-120 days prior to permit expiration.
- Applicants must include a non-refundable payment of $50.00 (certified check, cashier's check, or money order) made payable to SLED.
- Applicants must submit a good quality photocopy of their state issued driver's license or officially issued identification card.
- Resident aliens must provide a copy of their alien card from the Department of Homeland Security.
- Qualified nonresident applicants must submit a completed Real Property Tax Form (SLED Form R-168).

The following only apply to NEW permit applications:

- Applicants must submit an _original_ completed, signed, and dated application. The CWP instructor must also sign the application.
- Applicants must submit two (2) complete, legible sets of fingerprint cards.
- Active duty military applicants must submit military orders. Retired or former military applicants must submit a copy of their DD214.
- Retired law enforcement officers exempt from paying the fee must submit proof of retirement benefits/pension documentation.
- Active/retired South Carolina law enforcement officers exempt from training must submit current legal and firearm training documentation. Out-of-state retired law enforcement officers (or those whose certification has expired) must submit proof of graduation from a federal or state academy that included firearms training as a graduation requirement.
- Disabled veterans exempt from paying the fee must submit documentation from the VA indicating disability percentage.
- CWP training courses must have been completed within three years of filing the application.
- Training date, instructor certification number, and student number must be entered onto the application.
- You must submit a signed copy of the SLED CWP Instructor/Student Checklist with your application.

CERTIFICATION OF INFORMATION BY APPLICANT:

- I am eligible for a South Carolina Concealed Weapon Permit pursuant to Sections 23-31-210/215 of the S.C. Code of Laws.
- I am not prohibited from possessing a handgun pursuant to Section 922, Title 18, United States Code.
- I will notify SLED immediately if I become prohibited by federal/state laws or court orders from possessing a handgun.
- I acknowledge false information may cause denial of my application and subject me to any applicable criminal penalties.
- My signature certifies I have reviewed the entire application and all information on it is true and correct.

Signature of Applicant: _____ Date: _____

Form R-078 (Revised 3/4/2014)

CONCEALED WEAPON PERMITS SECTION 23-31-210

"Law Abiding Citizens Self-Defense Act of 1996"

(1) "Resident" means an individual who is present in South Carolina with the intention of making a permanent home in South Carolina or military personnel on permanent change of station orders.

(2) "Qualified nonresident" means an individual who owns real property in South Carolina, but who resides in another state.

(3) "Picture identification" means:

(a) a valid driver's license or photographic identification card issued by the state in which the applicant resides; or

(b) an official photographic identification card issued by the Department of Revenue, a federal or state law enforcement agency, an agency of the United States Department of Defense, or the United States Department of State.

(4) "Proof of training" means an original document or certified copy of the document supplied by an applicant that certifies that he is either:

(a) a person who, within three years before filing an application, successfully has completed a basic or advanced handgun education course offered by a state, county, or municipal law enforcement agency or a nationally recognized organization that promotes gun safety. This education course must include, but is not limited to:

(i) information on the statutory and case law of this State relating to handguns and to the use of deadly force;

(ii) information on handgun use and safety;

(iii) information on the proper storage practice for handguns with an emphasis on storage practices that reduces the possibility of accidental injury to a child; and

(iv) the actual firing of the handgun in the presence of the instructor;

(b) a person who demonstrates any of the following must comply with the provisions of subitem (a)(i) only:

(i) a person who demonstrates the completion of basic military training provided by any branch of the United States military who produces proof of his military service through the submission of a DD214 form;

(ii) a retired law enforcement officer who produces proof that he is a graduate of the Criminal Justice Academy or that he was a law enforcement officer prior to the requirement for graduation from the Criminal Justice Academy; or

(iii) a retired state or federal law enforcement officer who produces proof of graduation from a federal or state academy that includes firearms training as a graduation requirement;

(c) an instructor certified by the National Rifle Association or another SLED-approved competent national organization that promotes the safe use of handguns;

(d) a person who can demonstrate to the Director of SLED or his designee that he has a proficiency in both the use of handguns and state laws pertaining to handguns;

(e) an active duty police handgun instructor;

(f) a person who has a SLED-certified or approved competitive handgun shooting classification; or

(g) a member of the active or reserve military, or a member of the National Guard.

SLED shall promulgate (publicize) regulations containing general guidelines for courses and qualifications for instructors which would satisfy the requirements of this item.

For purposes of sub-items (a) and (c), "proof of training" is not satisfied unless the organization and its instructors meet or exceed the guidelines and qualifications contained in the regulations promulgated by SLED pursuant to this item.

(5) "Concealable weapon" means a firearm having a length of less than twelve inches measured along its greatest dimension that must be carried in a manner that is hidden from public view in normal wear of clothing except when needed for self-defense, defense of others, and the protection of real or personal property.

(6) "Proof of ownership of real property" means a certified current document from the county assessor of the county in which the property is located verifying ownership of the real property. SLED must determine the appropriate document that fulfills this requirement.

ISSUANCE OF PERMITS -   SECTION 23-31-215

Notwithstanding any other provision of law, except subject to subsection (B), SLED must issue a permit, which is no larger than three and one-half inches by three inches in size, to carry a concealable weapon to a resident or qualified nonresident who is at least twenty-one years of age and who is not prohibited by state law from possessing the weapon upon submission of:

(1) a completed application signed by the person;

(2) a photocopy of a driver's license or photographic identification card;

(3) proof of residence or if the person is a qualified nonresident, proof of ownership of real property in this State;

(4) proof of actual or corrected vision rated at 20/40 within six months of the date of application or, in the case of a person licensed to operate a motor vehicle in this State, presentation of a valid driver's license;

(5) proof of training;

(6) payment of a fifty-dollar application fee. This fee must be waived for disabled veterans and retired law enforcement officers; and

7) a complete set of fingerprints unless, because of a medical condition verified in writing by a licensed medical doctor, a complete set of fingerprints is impossible to submit. In lieu of the submission of fingerprints, the applicant must submit the written statement from a licensed medical doctor specifying the reason or reasons why the applicant's fingerprints may not be taken. If all other qualifications are met, the Chief of SLED may waive the fingerprint requirements of this item. The statement of medical limitation must be attached to the copy of the application retained by SLED.

(B) Upon submission of the items required by subsection (A), SLED must conduct or facilitate a local, state, and federal fingerprint review of the applicant. SLED also must conduct a background check of the applicant through notification to and input from the sheriff of the county where the applicant resides or if the applicant is a qualified nonresident, where the applicant owns real property in this State. The sheriff within ten working days after notification by SLED, may submit a recommendation on an application. Before making a determination whether or not to issue a permit under this article, SLED must consider the recommendation provided pursuant to this subsection. If the fingerprint review and background check are favorable, SLED must issue the permit.

(C) SLED shall issue a written statement to an unqualified applicant specifying its reasons for denying the application within ninety days from the date the application was received; otherwise, SLED shall issue a concealable weapon permit. If an applicant is unable to comply with the provisions of Section 23-31-210(4), SLED shall offer the applicant a handgun training course that satisfies the requirements of Section 23-31-210(4). The course shall cost fifty dollars.

SLED shall use the proceeds to defray the training course's operating costs. If a permit is granted by operation of law because an applicant was not notified of a denial within the ninety-day notification period, the permit may be revoked upon written notification from SLED that sufficient grounds exist for revocation or initial denial.

(D) Denial of an application may be appealed. The appeal must be in writing and state the basis for the appeal. The appeal must be submitted to the Chief of SLED within thirty days from the date the denial notice is received. The chief shall issue a written decision within ten days from the date the appeal is received. An adverse decision shall specify the reasons for upholding the denial and may be reviewed by the Administrative Law Court pursuant to Article 5, Chapter 23, Title 1, upon a petition filed by an applicant within thirty days from the date of delivery of the division's decision.

(E) SLED must make permit application forms available to the public. A permit application form shall require an applicant to supply:

(1) name, including maiden name if applicable;

(2) date and place of birth;

(3) sex;

(4) race;

(5) height;

(6) weight;

(7) eye and hair color;

(8) current residence address; and

(9) all residence addresses for the three years preceding the application date.

(F) The permit application form shall require the applicant to certify that:

(1) he is not a person prohibited under state law from possessing a weapon;

(2) he understands the permit is revoked and must be surrendered immediately to SLED if the permit holder becomes a person prohibited under state law from possessing a weapon; and

(3) all information contained in his application is true and correct to the best of his knowledge.

(G) Medical personnel, law enforcement agencies, organizations offering handgun education courses pursuant to Section 23-31-210(4), and their personnel, who in good faith provide information regarding a person's application, must be exempt from liability that may arise from issuance of a permit; provided, however, a weapons instructor must meet the requirements established in Section 23-31-210(4) in order to be exempt from liability under this subsection.

(H) A permit application must be submitted in person, by mail, or online to SLED headquarters which shall verify the legibility and accuracy of the required documents. If an applicant submits his application online, SLED may continue to make all contact with that applicant through online communications.

(I) SLED must maintain a list of all permit holders and the current status of each permit. SLED may release the list of permit holders or verify an individual's permit status only if the request is made by a law enforcement agency to aid in an official investigation, or if the list is required to be released pursuant to a subpoena or court order. SLED may charge a fee not to exceed its costs in releasing the information under this subsection. Except as otherwise provided in this subsection, a person in possession of a list of permit holders obtained from SLED must destroy the list.

(J) A permit is valid statewide unless revoked because the person has:

(1) become a person prohibited under state law from possessing a weapon;

(2) moved his permanent residence to another state and no longer owns real property in this State;

(3) voluntarily surrendered the permit; or

(4) been charged with an offense that, upon conviction, would prohibit the person from possessing a firearm. However, if the person subsequently is found not guilty of the offense, then his permit must be reinstated at no charge.

Once a permit is revoked, it must be surrendered to a sheriff, police department, a SLED agent, or by certified mail to the Chief of SLED. A person who fails to surrender his permit in accordance with this subsection is guilty of a misdemeanor and, upon conviction, must be fined twenty-five dollars.

(K) A permit holder must have his permit identification card in his possession whenever he carries a concealable weapon. When carrying a concealable weapon pursuant to Article 4, Chapter 31, Title 23, a permit holder must inform a law enforcement officer of the fact that he is a permit holder and present the permit identification card when an officer:

(1) identifies himself as a law enforcement officer; and

(2) requests identification or a driver's license from a permit holder.

A permit holder must immediately report the loss or theft of a permit identification card to SLED headquarters. A person who violates the provisions of this subsection is guilty of a misdemeanor and, upon conviction, must be fined twenty-five dollars.

(L) SLED shall issue a replacement for lost, stolen, damaged, or destroyed permit identification cards after the permit holder has updated all information required in the original application and the payment of a five-dollar replacement fee. Any change of permanent address must be communicated in writing to SLED within ten days of the change accompanied by the payment of a fee of five dollars to defray the cost of issuance of a new permit. SLED shall then issue a new permit with the new address.

A permit holder's failure to notify SLED in accordance with this subsection constitutes a misdemeanor punishable by a twenty-five dollar fine. The original permit shall remain in force until receipt of the corrected permit identification card by the permit holder, at which time the original permit must be returned to SLED.

QUALIFIED NON-RESIDENT FORM

If you reside in another state, yet have ownership of real estate in South Carolina you may qualify as a qualified non-resident for permitting purposes. You must have legal ownership in a parcel of land located in South Carolina, even if it's only a small percentage of ownership interest.

SOUTH CAROLINA LAW ENFORCEMENT DIVISION

NIKKI R. HALEY
Governor

MARK A. KEEL
Chief

South Carolina Non-Resident Concealed Weapon Permit (CWP)
Real Property Tax Form

I, _____, in my official capacity as Assessor of _____

_____ County, South Carolina, hereby certify that the records of this

Assessor's Office indicate that _____ (non-resident

CWP applicant pursuant to S.C. Code Section 23-31-215(A)(3)) currently owns real property in

this county, more specifically described as_____

_____(address of property), TMS #_____ (Tax Map Number).

_____
Printed name and signature of Assessor

_____
Date

Form R-168
4/14

To establish proof of ownership in the real property, an applicant must submit a completed SOUTH CAROLINA NON-RESIDENT CONCEALED WEAPON PERMIT REAL PROPERTY TAX FORM (SLED Form R-168) to SLED along with the application, completed fingerprint cards, proof of training, copy of ID and the application fee of $50.00.

Form R-168 must be completed by the county tax assessor of the county in which the property is located. Form R-168 can be obtained from SLED's website: http://www.sled.sc.gov/

WAIVER OF APPLICATION FEE

Under South Carolina law SECTION 23-31-215 (A)(6), if you are a retired police officer or a disabled veteran of the U.S. Armed Forces you are exempt from the $50.00 application fee.

To document your status as a retired police officer, you must submit a letter from the department from which you retired or the retirement system which pays your benefits.

To document status as a disabled veteran, you must submit a letter from the US Veteran Administration or a notarized copy of another official document, such as a DD-214 certifying your status as a disabled veteran.

CRIMINAL RECORD

SLED's new CWP application (Revised 03/4/2014) is a little less intrusive than its earlier predecessors in regards to criminal history. There are only three qualifying questions.

Are you a South Carolina resident or qualified non-resident?
___Yes ___ No

Have you successfully completed the required training?
___Yes ___ No

Are you allowed by all applicable federal/state laws and court orders to possess a handgun?
___Yes ___ No

Your truthful answers must be "YES". If you answer "NO" to either question you are not eligible for a permit.

You are required to sign and date the application certifying that all information is true and correct, subject to perjury. Submitting false information on your application form is a crime for which you can be prosecuted. In addition to the above question, you will have to sign a Certification of Information by Applicant.

- I am eligible for a South Carolina Concealed Weapons Permit pursuant to Section 23-31-210/215, SC Code of Laws.
- I am not prohibited from possessing a handgun pursuant to Section 922, Title 18, United States Code.
- I will notify SLED immediately if I become prohibited by federal/state laws or court orders from possessing a handgun.
- I acknowledge false information may cause denial of my application and subject me to any applicable criminal penalties.
- My signature certifies I have reviewed the entire application and all information on it is true and correct.

Any past convictions of minor crimes may not disqualify you from being issued a carry permit, but your <u>failure to report a criminal history will</u>.

FINGERPRINTS

Another reason for rejection of applications is that the fingerprints which have been submitted are not classifiable. The FBI has strict standards governing criminal record information, even to other law enforcement agencies. SLED will not proceed to conduct a complete criminal record check if your FBI fingerprint card displays unclassifiable fingerprints.

If your fingerprints do not show the complete pattern area of all of your fingers, from one side of the fingernail to the other, with no smudges or blots, the card will be rejected by the FBI and returned to you, non-processed.

It makes no difference whether you have been fingerprinted before, it will take 40-70 days for the FBI to reject unclassifiable fingerprints.

APPLICATION PROCESSING TIME

The time taken to process your application primarily depends upon the time needed by the FBI to perform national criminal record checks using your fingerprints. SLED usually receives the FBI report back within 40-70 days.

The law requires that SLED issue a permit or the applicant notified of denial within 90 days from the date the application is received for processing. If more than 90 days has passed since your application was mailed, you may want to call SLED Regulatory Services at (803) 896-7015.

SLED will process your application as quickly as possible. You should give them no less than 90 days before calling to follow-up on your application.

NOW AVAILABLE

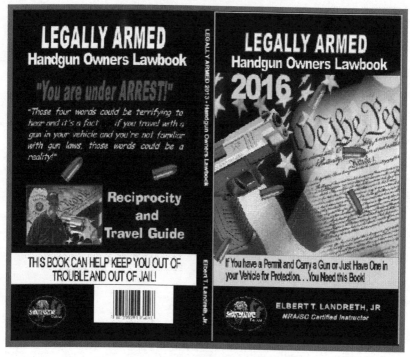

www.shooterszone.com

Chapter 3

SOUTH CAROLINA
Statutory and Case Law

Carrying a concealed weapon is an important undertaking and must always be taken extremely seriously. <u>It can change your life as you now know it, for better or worse, the choice is yours</u>.

You must be thoroughly familiar with your firearm, with federal and state firearm laws, and with the rules and regulations governing the carrying of a concealed weapon.

The legality of carrying a concealed weapon is a complex issue, and in this chapter you will learn exactly what South Carolina law means in regards to being legally armed.

Federal and state laws consider a gun, even an unloaded gun, to be a deadly weapon, a deadly weapon that can kill or inflict serious bodily injury to a human being. For that reason it is important that you understand and have a reasonable degree of knowledge of what is and what is not allowed according to the federal and state laws.

SECTION 16-3-10 of the South Carolina Criminal Code defines "Murder" as the killing of any person with malice aforethought, either expressed or implied. It further refers to a "homicide," as the killing of one human being by another.

Not all homicides are considered criminal acts of murder. A military serviceman may be forced to take the life of an enemy soldier in times of conflict or war, a police officer may be forced to shoot and even kill a criminal caught while in the commission of a violent crime.

Many times, people are involved in accidents which are considered unavoidable, in which another individual loses his life, and generally speaking, criminal charges do not result from those type incidents. There are numerous circumstances in which a person injures or even kills another, and by law the act will be ruled justified by the courts. *The means in which these homicides take place are called criminal defenses, acts by which a person can defend himself from criminal prosecution.*

More specifically, *criminal defenses* are referred to as *self-defense, defense of third parties, defense of property* and the *defense of habitation*; this means the act of protecting yourself, others, your home and your possessions. Each of these four criminal defenses has somewhat different standards, and <u>you must be familiar with each of them.</u>

Self-defense is considered by most people to be the primary justification defense, and it is perhaps the most common or familiar of all defenses. Understanding the principles of self-defense is essential to gaining the knowledge of the justification defenses.

The purpose of this chapter is to very plainly and simply present the elements of self-defense to the concealed weapon permit applicant, or other individual who may be concerned about the legalities of personal protection. Even a person who is new to the study of the criminal defenses should be comfortable reading and studying this section.

Throughout history, federal and state laws have recognized the rights of individuals to protect themselves from unjustified attacks, cases in which individuals might otherwise fall victim of an assault and battery, or even more tragic, a homicide.

Although we frequently hear the words *assault and battery* used in conjunction in criminal cases, they are actually two entirely different offenses. The term *assault* refers to a threat of harm, a threat where one person tries to physically harm another in a way that makes the person under attack feel immediately threatened. The laws consider such threats as offensive *touching,* for example, a hard shove, a slap, a punch, and even in more violent situations, a blow from a club, a stab from a knife, or even a shot from a gun. On the other hand, actual physical contact is not always necessary for an act to be considered a criminal offense; threatening gestures that would alarm or frighten a reasonable and prudent person can constitute an assault.

Some degree of touching, bumping and shoving is experienced and expected in our daily lives. Someone may accidently bump into another person in church or in an office hallway, but we're not referring to those simple and in most cases innocent accidents, we're referring to a much more serious action, an *unjustified action*, an action constituting an intentional assault of one person by another.

Assault is the threat of intentional harm, and *battery* is the actual carrying out of the threat, the physical act of hitting, shoving, pushing, stabbing or shooting.

A person is protected by law from such intentional physical abuse, and that person has the right to protect himself from such unlawful attacks, provided that he is acting in a manner which is consistent to the requirements set forth in the South Carolina code of laws relating to self-defense.

The case of *South Carolina V. Fuller*, (1989), sets precedent for the elements of a plea of self-defense in the State of South Carolina.

A citizen is justified in using deadly force in self-defense if the following elements are present.

The person must be without any fault in bringing on the difficulty;

The person must actually believe that he or she is in imminent danger of loss of life or serious bodily injury or was actually in such danger;

If the person did believe that he or she was in such danger, a person of ordinary average prudence, caution or courage would have believed himself to be in such danger;

The person had no other possible means of avoiding serious bodily injury or from losing his own life than to act as he did in that particular situation.

If the person actually was in such danger, the circumstances were such as would warrant a person of ordinary average prudence (prudence is defined as the ability to govern and discipline oneself by the use of reason), caution or courage to strike the fatal blow in order to save himself from serious bodily injury or from losing his own life;

It doesn't really matter how you as an individual may perceive a particular situation, or how you may tend to interpret the law, the important thing to remember is how a person of ordinary average prudence, caution or courage would view the situation. This simply means that subjective individual standards or opinions are not important and do not apply in a court of criminal law.

The person claiming self-defense is not the sole judge of the necessity for the act. The courts must look through the eyes of a reasonable person and judge on those standards. The bottom line is, would an ordinary person of average prudence, caution or courage believe that actions taken in a particular situation were necessary to prevent harm to the person claiming self-defense?

As previously stated, in order for a person to have the right to claim self-defense, he or she must actually believe that he is in imminent danger of serious bodily injury or loss of life, or was at that instant in such danger. The word . . . *imminent* means *right now, impending, and forthcoming,* it does not refer to some future date or time.

Although a person may be confident in his ability to safely defend himself from an attacker and may not necessarily fear his assailant, he must feel reasonably sure that the attack is inevitable, it is forthcoming and that it is reasonable to defend himself.

In *South Carolina vs. Fuller*, the defendant has the right to act on appearances in the plea of self-defense. You <u>do not</u> have to actually see a weapon in the hand of an attacker, or even on his person. The claim of self-defense would be considered justified as long as a *reasonable and prudent person* would have entertained the same thought; they would have believed that the attacker did have a firearm or other dangerous weapon at the time of the attack.

Assume that an attacker grabbed the person claiming self-defense by the throat and stated that he was going to "take care of him." The attacker then reached into the toolbox of his truck and produced an object that appeared shiny; the victim believed the object was a gun. The victim did not see a gun, but he did believe it to be a gun, and at that instant, the victim shot the attacker. It was later determined that the shiny object was something other than a firearm or weapon.

Would a reasonable and prudent person have acted in the same manner? Should the defendant have waited until he could positively identify the object as a firearm or other dangerous weapon?

If the defendant in this case had waited to be absolutely sure that the attacker did have a weapon, such as a gun, knife or club, it possibly could have been the defendants last living act.

After taking into consideration the legal precedence set by *South Carolina v. Fuller*, in this case, the courts would have found it reasonable for the person to act in self-defense, and his actions would be ruled justified.

In the above case scenario, we have *words accompanied by actions*. Words alone, no matter how outrageous or insulting will never justify the taking of another person's life. However, words of a threatening nature accompanied by hostile acts <u>may</u> establish the justification for self-defense.

The important thing to remember is that the action would be considered justified, only if a *reasonable and prudent person* would have had the same belief, and would have taken the same actions.

REASONABLE RESPONDING FORCE

In response to the threat of danger, the force employed by a victim must be <u>*reasonable*</u> and <u>*proportionate*</u> to the threatening force. It may be reasonable to respond to a non-deadly attack, such as a shove or slap with force of a similar nature, likewise, it may be reasonable to respond with deadly force in defense from an attacker who is using a club, a knife or a gun, but rarely is it considered reasonable to respond to a non-deadly attack with deadly force.

Courts have ruled that even an unloaded gun could be used to beat or strike, therefore, <u>whether a gun is used for shooting or clubbing, it is still going to be viewed by the courts as a deadly weapon</u>. Before using deadly force in response to an attack, you should always be sure that the elements of self-defense are present and in your favor. You should be sure that the actions which you are taking would be considered justified by a *reasonable and prudent person.*

HOW MUCH FORCE IS CONSIDERED REASONABLE?

The amount of force which will be deemed justifiable will depend on the circumstances. The law states that a person may use only the amount of force as is necessary for his or her deliverance, and only such force that is necessary to repel the attack and no more.

Deadly force may be used only in response to deadly force. That person may respond with force and may continue to use force only as long as a threat continues. The defendant need not retreat unless he knows he can retreat with complete safety.

In one prominent case, the defendant claimed to have shot his attacker four times at close range with a shotgun, and the defendant was found by the court to have acted reasonably. When a person is justified in the use of deadly force, he is also justified with the continued use of deadly force <u>until the threat of harm is eliminated</u>.

JUSTIFICATION OF FORCE –

When the threat of danger no longer exists, neither does your justification to continue to use force. For example, after being shot the attacker collapsed unconscious, the person claiming self-defense would not have legal justification to continue shooting the assailant.

A *reasonable and prudent person* would realize that the threat of danger no longer existed, therefore further actions by the defendant would not be warranted, and the plea of self-defense would not be available.

The guidelines for the third element of self-defense is simple; a person claiming self-defense must be without fault in bringing on the attack and must have no other reasonable means of avoiding the attack, except to act as he did. This means that the defendant cannot have been the initial aggressor, the plea of self-defense will not be available if he started the fight, even if the claim is based upon being spoken too insultingly. Remember, words alone will not justify the need for self-defense.

A citizen is not without fault, and the plea of self-defense is unavailable if he/she voluntarily participates in mutual combat.

Deadly force may not be used to stop a simple assault.

One exception for example, Joe started a fight with Tom, simply pushing him around, using non-deadly force, but still the initial aggressor. Tom responds by delivering deadly force with a gun. Although Joe was the initial aggressor, he started the argument; Tom elevated the level of aggression by introducing a deadly weapon into the conflict. Joe then killed Tom with a single shot from his .38 caliber handgun.

How would a *reasonable and prudent person* judge that situation? If Joe started the argument and Tom elevated the level of aggression to that of deadly force, Joe would be justified in defending himself with the means necessary to repel the attack. The defending force may be deadly force only in response to attackers' deadly force.

Looking further into this fictional altercation, let's say that Joe, who was the initial aggressor, managed to get away without any bodily injury or the use of deadly force, hoping that Tom would cool-off and the matter would just blow over. Then later in the evening, Tom shows up and restarts the fight making threatening remarks and brandishing a handgun. Believing that he was in imminent danger of serious bodily injury or even loss of life Joe shot and killed Tom.

How would a <u>reasonable and prudent person</u> judge that situation?

Joe was out on the town minding his own business and hoping that Tom would not show up and be a problem. Tom shows up running his mouth, making threats and brandishing a handgun. It appears that Joe would be justified in using self-defense because of the escalating nature of the altercation, whereby, words and hostile acts may, depending on the circumstances, establish a plea of self-defense.

NO DUTY TO RETREAT -

Prior to June 9, 2006, a person claiming self-defense in South Carolina had a fourth element to consider, and that was a *duty to retreat*. The law stated that a person had the *duty to retreat* before using deadly force in self-defense on a public street or highway, even when in his or her own vehicle.

You could not claim self-defense when using deadly force against an attack in public. Some felt that the idea of retreating from a confrontation might show a sign of weakness, but the law considered it a show of good sense. South Carolina courts felt that *"wounded feelings would heal, but dead bodies would not."* Law makers believed that if you could safely retreat from a criminal confrontation, you should retreat from the conflict and leave the area.

It seemed a somewhat ludicrous, but the law to required that a person retreat from a confrontation while in public areas; streets, a parking lots, buildings open to the public, even if the person was the victim and was in the right.

There were a few exceptions, for example; In the case of *South Carolina v. McGee*, (1937), *"One need not retreat if to do so would apparently increase his danger."* The threat of harm would have been greatly intensified, therefore, if retreating would have placed you at risk of serious bodily injury or loss of life, under the law, <u>the duty retreat was not required</u> to be able to claim self-defense.

THE CASTLE DOCTRINE -

The **Castle Doctrine** referred to as the *'Protection of Persons and Property Act'* was signed into law June 9, 2006 by South Carolina Governor Mark Sanford. The Castle Doctrine, a common law, recognizes that <u>a person's home is his castle</u> and extends the person's right of self-defense to include an <u>occupied vehicle</u> and the <u>person's place of business</u>.

The Castle Doctrine provides for law-abiding citizens to protect themselves, their families, and others from intruders and attackers <u>without fear of prosecution or civil action</u> for acting in defense of themselves and others.

The South Carolina Constitution, Section 20, Article 1 guarantees a citizen the right to bear arms and that right shall not be infringed. The law further recognizes that persons residing in or visiting this State have the right to expect to remain unmolested and safe within their homes, businesses, and vehicles.

The law recognizes that no person or victim of crime should be required to surrender his personal safety to a criminal, nor should a person or victim be required to needlessly retreat in the face of intrusion or attack.

The law defines the term 'Dwelling' as being a building or conveyance of any kind, including an attached porch, whether the building or conveyance is temporary or permanent, mobile or immobile, which has a roof over it, including a tent, and is designed to be occupied by people lodging there at night.

The law defines the term 'Great bodily injury' as bodily injury which creates a substantial risk of death or which causes serious, permanent disfigurement, or protracted loss or impairment of the function of a bodily member or organ.

The law defines the term 'Residence' as a dwelling in which a person resides either temporarily or permanently or is visiting as an invited guest.

The law defines a 'Vehicle' as a conveyance of any kind, whether or not motorized, which is designed to transport people or property.

PRESUMPTION OF REASONABLE FEAR -

Under South Carolina law, Section 16-11-440,(A) a person is presumed to have a reasonable fear of imminent peril of death or great bodily injury to himself or another person when using deadly force that is intended or likely to cause death or great bodily injury to another person;

(a) if the person against whom the deadly force is used is in the process of unlawfully and forcefully entering,

(b) or has unlawfully and forcibly entered a dwelling, residence, or occupied vehicle,

(c) or if he removes or is attempting to remove another person against his will from the dwelling, residence, or occupied vehicle;

(d) or who uses deadly force knows or has reason to believe that an unlawful and forcible entry or unlawful and forcible act is occurring or has occurred.

(B) (1) The presumption provided in subsection (A) does not apply if the person against whom the deadly force is used has the right to be in or is a lawful resident of the dwelling, residence, or occupied vehicle including, but not limited to, an owner, lessee, or titleholder.

(B)(2) The presumption provided in subsection (A) does not apply if the person sought to be removed is a child or grandchild, or is otherwise in the lawful custody or under the lawful guardianship, of the person against whom the deadly force is used.

(B)(3) The presumption provided in subsection (A) does not apply if the person who uses deadly force is engaged in an unlawful activity or is using the dwelling, residence, or occupied vehicle to further an unlawful activity.

(B)(4) The presumption provided in subsection (A) does not apply if the person against whom the deadly force is used is a law enforcement officer who enters or attempts to enter a dwelling, residence, or occupied vehicle in the performance of his official duties, and he identifies himself in accordance with applicable law or the person using force knows or reasonably should have known that the person entering or attempting to enter is a law enforcement officer.

(C) A person who is not engaged in an unlawful activity and who is attacked in another place where he has a right to be, including, but not limited to, his place of business, has no duty to retreat and has the right to *STAND HIS GROUND* and meet force with force, including deadly force, if he reasonably believes it is necessary to prevent death or great bodily injury to himself or another person or to prevent the commission of a violent crime as defined in Section 16-1-60.

(D) A person who unlawfully and by force enters or attempts to enter a person's dwelling, residence, or occupied vehicle is presumed to be doing so with the intent to commit an unlawful act involving force or a violent crime as defined in Section 16-1-60.

(E) A person who by force enters or attempts to enter a dwelling, residence, or occupied vehicle in violation of an order of protection, restraining order, or condition of bond is presumed to be doing so with the intent to commit an unlawful act regardless of whether the person is a resident of the dwelling, residence, or occupied vehicle including, but not limited to, an owner, lessee, or titleholder.

For purposes of defining South Carolina law, a violent crime includes the offenses of murder, criminal sexual conduct in the first and second degree, criminal sexual conduct with minors, first and second degree, assault with intent to commit criminal sexual conduct, first and second degree, assault and battery with intent to kill, kidnapping, voluntary manslaughter, armed robbery, attempted armed robbery, carjacking, drug trafficking or trafficking cocaine base, manufacturing or trafficking methamphetamine, arson in the first or second degree, burglary in the first or second degree, engaging a child for a sexual performance, homicide by child abuse, aiding and abetting homicide by child abuse, inflicting great bodily injury upon a child, allowing great bodily injury to be inflicted upon a child, criminal domestic violence of a high and aggravated nature, abuse or neglect of a vulnerable adult resulting in death, abuse or neglect of a vulnerable adult resulting in great bodily injury, accessory before the fact to commit any of the above offenses, attempt to commit any of the above offenses, and taking of a hostage by an inmate. Only the above criminal offenses specifically listed in this section are considered violent offenses.

IMMUNITY FROM CRIMINAL PROSECUTION -

A person who uses deadly force as permitted by the provisions of this article or another applicable provision of law is <u>justified in using deadly force</u> and is <u>immune from criminal prosecution and civil action</u> for the use of deadly force, unless the person against whom deadly force was used is a law enforcement officer acting in the performance of his official duties and he identifies himself in accordance with applicable law or the person using deadly force knows or reasonably should have known that the person is a law enforcement officer. (Section 16-11-450)

A law enforcement agency may use standard procedures for investigating the use of deadly force as described in subsection (A), <u>but the agency may not arrest the person for using deadly force unless probable cause exists that the deadly force used was unlawful.</u>

The court shall award reasonable attorneys' fees, court costs, compensation for loss of income, and all expenses incurred by the defendant in defense of a civil action brought by a plaintiff <u>if the court finds that the defendant is immune from prosecution</u> as provided in this subsection.

THE DEFENSE OF HABITATION

The *Law Abiding Citizens Self-Defense Act of 1996* has provisions to deal with confrontations between a homeowner and a guest or trespasser which might result in the use of deadly force by one party or the other.

The law anticipates that the individual who is present on another person's property could be legally armed (concealed weapon permit holder), under this law, and the law says that the provisions of this act do not change the law with respect to the potential liability in such situations.

Should the homeowner attack his guest, the guest must make every attempt possible to safely retreat, even though the dispute was no initiated by the guest. If the guest believes beyond any doubt that he cannot safely retreat without the risk of serious bodily injury or death, then and only then should he or she act in self-defense, using only such force which is necessary for his deliverance from the situation. The same self-defense rule discussed earlier applies.

Would an ordinary person of average prudence, caution or courage believe that the actions taken under the particular circumstances were necessary to prevent harm to the person claiming self-defense?

If the answer is yes, the court must find the defendant justified in his actions.

"A man is no more bound to allow himself to be run out of his rest room than his workshop." You do not have the legal justification to exercise deadly force just because someone trespasses onto your property, however, a property owner may shoot a trespasser with impunity where the incursion on the owners property is also accompanied by a threat of personal harm to the owner, his family or others who he is entitled to defend. The right to use force in the defense of property is more limited than the right to use force to defend a human life.

If a thief forcibly breaks into your home at 2:00 A.M. in the morning, you <u>do not</u> have to conduct an interrogation to determine if the burglar means you any harm, by law you are not required to know whether or not the burglar is armed. You only need to be sure that it is not a family member or friend who has wondered into your home; otherwise, you are allowed to respond with deadly force.

The same elements apply to the use of self-defense in one's own place of business. In the absence of any fault on the part of the business owner, if there is an immediate danger of serious bodily harm or loss of life, whether actual or reasonably expected, a person may use such force as is necessary, however, proportional to the attacking force, to prevent serious bodily injury or loss of life.

- A citizen may use only such force which is necessary in the protection of his/her dwelling.

- The important question to always consider, "Would a reasonable and prudent person have taken the same action?"

How would a reasonable person respond under similar circumstances, and you should be able to provide the answer for yourself. You must believe that you or another is in immediate danger, and if that is the case, the defense of habitation may be used.

The law essentially declares that every human life is considered to be a precious being, even the life of a thief or felon, and therefore, it should be preserved, unless taking it is the only reasonable remedy.

That is an important reason why our society has applied unique safeguards in death penalty cases, and that is what a person must do in using self-defense. All other logical possibilities must be exhausted before the striking of a fatal blow.

DEFENSE OF OTHERS - THE ALTER EGO RULE –

South Carolina recognizes the *"alter-ego"* rule, also known as *"Defense of Others"* with respect to the defense of any relative, friend, or bystander in order to deter an unlawful or unjustified attack.

South Carolina has adopted what is called the ***alter ego rule*** with respect to the defense of *others*. In *South Carolina v. Cook*, (1907), the court summarized this rule:

[A] person who intervenes on behalf of another will not be allowed the benefit of the plea of self-defense, unless such pleas would have been available to the person whose part he took in case he himself had done the killing since the person interfering is affected by the principle that the party bringing on the difficulty cannot take advantage of his own wrong.

In *South Carolina v. Hays*, (1922) the Court approved a "defense of others" instruction. In such case, the right to take the life of such an assailant upon such unprovoked assault extends to any relative, friend, or bystander who would likewise have the right to take the life of such an assailant if such acts were necessary to save the person so wrongly assailed from imminent danger of being murdered by such assailant.

In other words, if the assailant makes a malicious and unprovoked assault with a deadly weapon upon one person with the apparent malicious intention to take the life of the person assailed and thereby commit murder, then, where the danger of the commission of such murder is imminent, any relative, friend, or bystander could have the right to take the life of such assailant if necessary, in order to prevent the commission of such murder, provided there was no other reasonable means of escape for the person being assailed, and provided both the person assailed and the people coming to his defense were without legal fault in bringing on the difficulty."

Under conditions set forth in the instructions, you can come to the rescue of a bystander, but here's a problem you may face. The question must be resolved as to whether the rescuer may rely on appearances, as you can do in self-defense. For example, if two individuals were in a heated skirmish you would probably go to the aid of the smaller or weaker party who just may be the initial aggressor, however innocently unknown by the rescuer. That's the way most persons would react to that type situation.

This means, if an individual "has the right to defend himself, then the intervening party is also protected by that same right." The person intervening is deemed to "*stand in the shoes*" of the person on whose behalf he is intervening.

If that individual "had the right to defend himself, then the intervening party is also protected by that right. If, however, the party had no right to use force . . . then the intervening party will also assume the liability of the person on whose behalf he intervened."

By law, the rescuer assumes all the rights and limitations of that person. If the person being rescued has a right to claim self-defense, so does his rescuer, but on the other hand, if the person being rescued has a duty to retreat, the same applies to his rescuer, and neither has a right of self-defense. The rules of "defense of others" apply to "any relative, friend or bystander *South Carolina v. Hays*, supra.

This rule of law may tend to reduce the number persons who might go to the rescue of others, but the same laws may decrease the number of innocent persons being injured or killed by a would-be-rescuer who mistakenly sided with the wrong party. Circumstances are not always as they appear, you must *be sure of the facts* before jumping into a confrontation involving others.

THE DEFENSE OF PROPERTY

The defense of property generally cannot be considered without also considering the defense of habitation, even though the rules pertaining to the two are distinctly different in important aspects, especially in the defense of habitation, they overlap with many other justification defenses.

In the case of *South Carolina v. Hibler*, (1907) the Court recognized that the general rule in the defense of property is that, only such force must be used as is necessary, or apparently necessary to a reasonably prudent man. Any greater expenditure of force cannot be considered justifiable, and will therefore result in criminal prosecution.

The weight of modern authority limits the use of deadly force in the defense of a dwelling to situations in which the homeowner/resident reasonably believes that the intruder intends to commit a felony, or only when the use of deadly force would be authorized by the law.

In reviewing the criminal defense, *the defense of property*, we are referring to personal property such as your car, stereo, VCR, watch, your money, etc. A person is allowed to use *reasonable force* to defend his property from theft or other interference and even recover it, if it has been criminally taken provided that it is an <u>immediate action</u> and the use of reasonable force necessitates the recovery.

One who is dispossessed of property has certain legal remedies available, but in no way is he or she justified in using force to re-enter or recapture property unless he has acted immediately after the taking of the property, or is actually in pursuit of the thief.

This means that you cannot wait for days to react to a situation; you are not justified in playing Chuck Norris and hunting down the thief who broke into your home, trying to recover your property.

The law provides that your response must be an immediate action, if your actions are otherwise, you may be subject to a criminal charge. If you can stop the theft and regain possession of your property by simply asking the person to stop, then no amount of force is considered reasonable. If a verbal command is appropriate, then the use of any physical force is not going to be justified.

Using force in defense of property requires essentially the same elements as that of self-defense, but with one profound difference, <u>deadly force is never justified if all that is at stake is property</u>.

Again, a human life is worth more than a TV, VCR or even an expensive automobile. However, if we add to this situation the criminal offense of armed robbery, and the threat is accompanied by a verbal threat to shoot, stab or club, which could result in serious injury or loss of life, then use of deadly force, will be justified.

Likewise, if you are running after a criminal who just stolen your TV or your wallet, and he turns and pulls a weapon such as knife, gun, tire tool, ball bat or any other instrument which could be used as a deadly weapon, the use of force would be considered self-defense, provided the returning force is proportionate to the threatening force.

If the requirements of self-defense are satisfied, given the right circumstances you may be justified in using deadly force, but the fact still remains, the right to use force in defense of property is more limited than the right to use force in defense of human life. The important thing to remember, would a reasonable and prudent man have taken the same action?

RESISTING A LAWFUL ARREST

At times, legally armed citizens for one reason or another find themselves to be victims of unfortunate circumstances, sometimes innocently, other times self-perpetrated, however both resulting with the same conclusion, arrest by the authorities. The incidence of arrest, the process of taking a person into custody, is usually carried out by a duly-appointed law enforcement officer.

Ordinarily, after following routine police procedures, and answering a few questions, the detained citizen will be free to go about his own way, unless serious criminal laws have been violated through the use of bad judgment, carelessness, stupidity, and there are occasions of an over-active temper.

A person may be arrested when there is probable cause to believe that he or she has committed a crime. In most cases, these arrests are made by police officers without warrants, they apprehend a suspect during the commission of a crime, or when they have sufficient reason to believe that a person is guilty of a criminal offense.

The important thing to remember is a citizen has no right to resist a lawful arrest. Even if you know that you are absolutely, positively 100% innocent of any charges, you still must surrender to the officer with no resistance.

Under South Carolina law SECTION 16-3-625, a *person who resists the lawful efforts of a law enforcement officer to arrest him or another person with the use or threat of use of a deadly weapon against the officer, and the person is in possession or claims to be in possession of a deadly weapon, is guilty of a felony and, upon conviction, must be punished by imprisonment for not more than ten nor less than two years.*

No sentence imposed hereunder for a first offense shall be suspended to less than six months nor shall the persons so sentenced be eligible for parole until after service of six months.

No person sentenced under this section for a second or subsequent offense shall have the sentence suspended to less than two years nor shall the person be eligible for parole until after service of two years.

CITIZENS ARREST

Our courts have established the rules of common law for a citizen's arrest by a private person (non-law enforcement). Under the guidelines set forth for modern common law, <u>a person who actually witnesses a felony being committed has a duty to attempt to arrest or detain the felon either personally or by calling others to his aid, or by seeking out a peace officer.</u>

The law also permits a private person to arrest a suspect for a felony which is not committed in his presence if, (1) a felony was actually committed and (2) the private person has reasonable cause to believe the person he is arresting has committed the felony for which the arrest is made. It is important to remember that <u>both</u> elements must be present.

If it is later determined that the person detained or arrested was innocent of the wrong doing, otherwise, he did not commit the felony for which he was arrested and the arrest is unlawful.

In addition, under state law the private citizen can arrest a person for a misdemeanor which is <u>committed in his presence</u>, if it constitutes a breach of the peace.

A private citizen does not have any rightful authority to arrest a person for a misdemeanor not committed in his presence.

With the exception of the witnessing of a felony actually being committed, the private citizen must give a reasonable notice of his purpose or intentions of an arrest, and the cause for the arrest, together with a demand that the suspect submit to the arrest.

If holding a suspect at gun-point, the Concealed Weapon Permit Holder is challenged by a Law Enforcement Officer, the CWP holder should do exactly as the officer says, not do anything that could be perceived by the officer as a threat, identify himself as a CWP holder and explain the situation to the officer.

NOW AVAILABLE

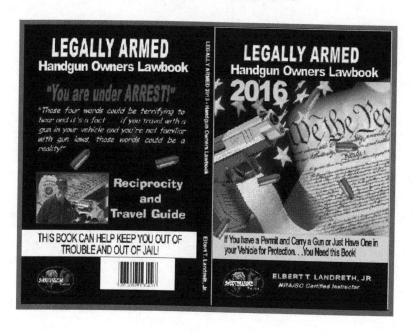
www.shooterszone.com

Chapter 4

BOOBY TRAPS
and
SPRING GUNS

Many TV programs, particular gangster movies, have shown a rifle or shotgun strapped to a chair and aimed at a doorway with a string or wire running from the firearm's trigger to the door knob. When the door opens . . . BANG!!!   The gun fires in the direction of the door and blast the unlucky one that opened the door. This type device is called a spring gun, booby trap, or a deadly mantrap and is illegal.

A frustrated homeowner who has been continually hassled by thieves may see this type of device as the answer to his needs, and decides to setup a similar trap at the probable point of entry. Here's the problem, a shotgun, rifle, handgun or other booby trap cannot differentiate the difference between a burglar, a neighbor or the kid next door.

In most all states, setting up such a device is a violation of the law, and if the device actually injures or causes loss of life, the person that set up the trap inevitably will face criminal charges. Here's proof from an international news service.

September 23, 1999

HOUMA, La. - A man who was apparently trying to break into a friend's mobile home was killed by a single bullet from a .22-caliber handgun which was rigged to go off when the front door opened.

The victim was a 37- year-old male, from rural Terrebonne Parish. A passer-by spotted his body Tuesday in front of the mobile home in HOUMA, La.

The owner of the mobile home was arrested on a manslaughter charge. He told investigators he had set up a booby trap before he left for work Tuesday because the home had been broken into four times in the past two weeks.

The County Sheriff said investigators who entered the mobile home found a nylon string reaching from the bottom of the front door to the trigger of the handgun. The home owner told authorities he put one bullet in the semi-automatic weapon on Tuesday morning.

"Thank God there was no clip or one of my officers could have been shot," the Sheriff said.

The Sheriff said the intruder was on his hands and knees when he broke in and was shot. The homeowner told investigators the trap was not set to kill, but to shoot an intruder in the legs.

The victim got into the home breaking through the bottom panel of the door, the Sheriff said.

Neighbors said the homeowner and the deceased man were friends. It was unclear why the man was trying to break into the home.

If the homeowner is convicted of manslaughter, he could receive 40 years in prison.

Placing a loaded trap gun, spring gun or like device is a violation of South Carolina code, SECTION 16-23-450,

It shall be unlawful for any person to construct, set or place a loaded trap gun, spring gun or any like device in any manner in any building or in any place within this State, and any violation of the provisions of this section shall constitute a misdemeanor and be punished by a fine of not less than one hundred dollars nor more than five hundred dollars or by imprisonment of not less than thirty days nor more than one year or by both fine and imprisonment, in the discretion of the court.

Booby traps cannot differentiate between good and evil, from right or wrong. Innocent people can be severely injured or even killed, don't take the chance . . . the risk is too great.

Chapter 5

UNITED STATES
CODE of LAW

Federal Firearm Laws

Interstate Transportation of Firearms

18 USC § 926A

Interstate Transportation of Firearms

Notwithstanding any other provision of any law or any rule or regulation of a State or any political subdivision thereof, any person who is not otherwise prohibited by this chapter from transporting, shipping, or receiving a firearm <u>shall be entitled to transport a firearm for any lawful purpose</u> from any place where he may lawfully possess and carry such firearm to any other place where he may lawfully possess and carry such firearm, if during such transportation the firearm is unloaded, and neither the firearm nor any ammunition being transported is readily accessible or is directly accessible from the passenger compartment of such transporting vehicle: Provided, that in the case of a vehicle without a compartment separate from the driver's compartment the firearm or ammunition shall be contained in a locked container other than the glove compartment or console.

The federal firearms transportation code (The Gun Control Act of 1968, Public Law 90-618) is the law guaranteeing law-abiding citizen a safe passage through states, counties and cities with restrictive or prohibitive firearm statues.

In actuality, this law guarantees that a citizen may legally transport a firearm from one locality where firearm possession is legal, through a location where laws may prohibit possession of a firearm, to another locality where possession is legal.

The following requirements must be met: (a) the firearm must be unloaded; (b) the firearm and any ammunition cannot be readily accessible to persons in the passenger compartment of the vehicle. The code does not specifically state the fact, but attorneys and legal scholars agree that the firearm and ammunition should be locked in the trunk of the vehicle, if so equipped. (c) If the vehicle has no separate storage compartment (trunk), the firearm and any ammunition must be stored in a locked storage box, other than the glove compartment or console.

The *Gun Control Act* does not specify that the locked box be placed in a location out of the reach of the vehicle operator or any passengers, it is strongly suggested by law enforcement officials that such action be taken. In the event that a vehicle is searched by law enforcement officers, it may possibly satisfy the authorities that you are taking all steps necessary to comply with the law and avert any legal actions or complications.

Please take note that transporting a firearm and carrying a firearm is totally different. Some states have made it practically impossible for the traveler to legally have a firearm readily available for his/her protection, or for the protection of their family. In those state, your only defense will be that you are transporting your firearm by virtue of the United States Code of Law 18 USC § 926A, *The Gun Control Act of 1968, Public Law 90-618.*

As previously stated, the intrastate traveler must be passing through the state and must be bound for a locality where the possession of such firearms is legal. Extended stops for reasons other than vehicle fueling or emergency services could possibly nullify the defense that the traveler was in fact transporting a firearm(s) under the requirements set forth in the United States Code of Law - 18 USC § 926, and cause the traveler to be subject to the effect of the laws of the state in question.

Chapter 6

FIREARMS ABOARD AIRCRAFT

FIREARMS ABOARD AIRCRAFT

CARRYING A WEAPON - - 49 USC Sec. 46303

(a) Civil Penalty. - An individual who, when on, or attempting to board, an aircraft in, or intended for operation in, air transportation or intrastate air transportation, has on or about the individual or the property of the individual a concealed dangerous weapon that is or would be accessible to the individual in flight is liable to the United States Government for a civil penalty of not more than $10,000 for each violation.

(b) Compromise and Set-off. - (1) The Secretary of Transportation may compromise the amount of a civil penalty imposed under subsection (a) of this section. (2) The Government may deduct the amount of a civil penalty imposed or compromised under this section from amounts it owes the individual liable for the penalty.

(c) Non-application. - This section does not apply to -

(1) a law enforcement officer of a State or political subdivision of a State, or an office or employee of the Government, authorized to carry arms in an official capacity; or

(2) another individual the Administrator of the Federal Aviation Administration by regulation authorizes to carry arms in an official capacity.

Carrying a weapon or explosive on an aircraft - 49 USC Sec. 46505

(a) Definition. - In this section, "loaded firearm" means a starter gun or a weapon designed or converted to expel a projectile through an explosive that has a cartridge, a detonator, or powder in the chamber, magazine, cylinder, or clip.

(b) General Criminal Penalty. - An individual shall be fined under title 18, imprisoned for not more than one year, or both, if the individual -

(1) when on, or attempting to get on, an aircraft in, or intended for operation in, air transportation or intrastate air transportation, has on or about the individual or the property of the individual a concealed dangerous weapon that is or would be accessible to the individual in flight;

(2) has placed, attempted to place, or attempted to have placed a loaded firearm on that aircraft in property not accessible to passengers in flight; or

(3) has on or about the individual, or has placed, attempted to place, or attempted to have placed on that aircraft, an explosive or incendiary device.

(c) Criminal Penalty Involving Disregard for Human Life. - An individual who willfully and without regard for the safety of human life, or with reckless disregard for the safety of human life, violates subsection (b) of this section, shall be fined under title 18, imprisoned for not more than 5 years, or both.

(d) Non-application. - Subsection (b)(1) of this section does not apply to-

(1) a law enforcement officer of a State or political subdivision of a State, or an officer or employee of the United States Government, authorized to carry arms in an official capacity;

(2) another individual the Administrator of the Federal Aviation Administration by regulation authorizes to carry a dangerous weapon in air transportation or intrastate air transportation; or

(3) an individual transporting a weapon (except a loaded firearm) in baggage not accessible to a passenger in flight if the air carrier was informed of the presence of the weapon.

FAA REGULATIONS - Sec. 108.11 Carriage of weapons

(a) No certificate holder required to conduct screening under a security program may permit any person to have, nor may any person have, on or about his or her person or property, a deadly or dangerous weapon, either concealed or unconcealed, accessible to him or her while aboard an airplane for which screening is required unless:

(1) The person having the weapon is:

(i) An official or employee of the United States, or a State or political subdivision of a State, or of a municipality who is authorized by his or her agency to have the weapon; or

(ii) Authorized to have the weapon by the certificate holder and the Administrator and has successfully completed a course of training in the use of firearms acceptable to the Administrator.

(2) The person having the weapon needs to have the weapon accessible in connection with the performance of his or her duty from the time he or she would otherwise check it in accordance with paragraph (d) of this section until the time it would be returned after deplaning.

(3) The certificate holder is notified;

(i) Of the flight on which the armed person intends to have the weapon accessible to him or her at least 1 hour, or in an emergency as soon as practicable, before departure; and

(ii) When the armed person is other than an employee or official of the United States, that there is a need for the weapon to be accessible to the armed person in connection with the performance of that person's duty from the time he or she would otherwise check it in accordance with paragraph (d) of this section until the time it would be returned to him or her after deplaning.

(4) The armed person identifies himself or herself to the certificate holder by presenting credentials that include his or her clear, full-face picture, his or her signature, and the signature of the authorizing official of his or her service or the official seal of his or her service.

A badge, shield, or similar may not be used as the sole means of identification.

(5) The certificate holder:

(i) Ensures that the armed person is familiar with its procedures for carrying a deadly or dangerous weapon aboard its airplane before the time the person boards the airplane;

(ii) Ensures that the identity of the armed person is known to each law enforcement officer and each employee of the certificate holder responsible for security during the boarding of the airplane; and

(iii) Notifies the pilot in command, other appropriate crew-members, and any other person authorized to have a weapon accessible to him or her aboard the airplane of the location of each authorized armed person aboard the airplane.

(b) No person may, while on board an airplane operated by a certificate holder for which screening is not conducted, carry on or about that person a deadly or dangerous weapon, either concealed or uncon-cealed.

This paragraph does not apply to:

(1) Officials or employees of a municipality or a State, or of the United States, who are authorized to carry arms; or

(2) Crew members and other persons authorized by the certificate holder to carry arms.

(c) No certificate holder may knowingly permit any person to transport, nor may any person transport or tender for transport, any explosive, incendiary or a loaded firearm in checked baggage aboard an airplane. For the purpose of this section, a loaded firearm means a firearm which has a live round of ammunition, cartridge, detonator, or powder in the chamber or in a clip, magazine, or cylinder inserted in it.

(d) No certificate holder may knowingly permit any person to transport, nor may any person transport or tender for transport, any unloaded firearm in checked baggage aboard an airplane unless:

(1) The passenger declares to the certificate holder, either orally or in writing before checking the baggage that any firearm carried in the baggage is unloaded;

(2) The firearm is carried in a container the certificate holder considers appropriate for air transportation;

(3) When the firearm is other than a shotgun, rifle, or other firearm normally fired from the shoulder position, the baggage in which it is carried is locked, and only the passenger checking the baggage retains the key or combination; and

(4) The baggage containing the firearm is carried in an area, other than the flight-crew compartment, that is inaccessible to Firearms aboard Aircraft passengers.

(e) No certificate holder may serve any alcoholic beverage to a person having a deadly or dangerous weapon accessible to him or her nor may such person drink any alcoholic beverage while aboard an airplane operated by the certificate holder.

(f) Paragraphs (a), (b), and (d) of this section do not apply to the carriage of firearms aboard air carrier flights conducted for the military forces of the Government of the United States when the total cabin load of the airplane is under exclusive use by those military forces if the following conditions are met:

(1) No firearm is loaded and all bolts to such firearms are locked in the open position; and

(2) The certificate holder is notified by the unit commander or officer in charge of the flight before boarding that weapons will be carried aboard the aircraft.

Chapter 7

HANDGUN SELECTION
Buying your first handgun . . .

Buying a handgun is a simple procedure and can be accomplished in relatively little time, however, due to the enormous responsibility of gun ownership it should be a well-thought out decision. Don't be in a rush to buy the first gun you see.

Be cautious as to recommendations in handgun selections from clerks at "sell-everything stores." Just because a person works at a business that sells guns does not necessarily make them a specialist in personal defense weapons.

Give it a lot of serious thought and if you can work it out, you should make arrangements to actually shoot as many different type handguns as possible prior to making your purchase. Talk to relatives and friends, anyone who you know that has some experience with the subject of guns. If possible, question your local law-enforcement officers as to their preference in personal defense weapons, I'm sure they would be happy to provide you with that information.

In choosing a handgun, you should consider your lifestyle and even how you dress. Will your wardrobe adequately adapt to the concealed carry of the handgun of your choosing? A concealed weapon permit, as the name implies, permits the applicant to carry a weapon, concealed on or about their person and it must be totally concealed from public view. Generally speaking, open carry of a handgun in the State of South Carolina is unlawful; however, there are some exceptions to the law.

Your choice of weapon and holster should be such as to be comfortable to wear or carry. If the weapon is burdensome and uncomfortable, chances are it won't take long for you to feel that concealed carry is too much trouble. Your physique and physical strength should play important parts in making a decision as to which handgun is best suited for you, as should be the size and geometry of your hands.

The size of the grip is an important consideration in choosing a handgun. When you are holding a handgun, your hand should fit comfortably and wrap around the handgun's grip panels. The grip panels should be long enough to adequately provide a resting place for your fingers. A handgun must feel comfortable and easily controllable for the shooter to safely and effectively handle the handgun.

The weight of your firearm and its physical size are important issues if you plan to carry it for long periods of time. In the long run, a smaller, lighter weight handgun may prove more comfortable, but you should not choose comfort over stopping power. The lack of power to put down an attacker could be more devastating than not being armed at all.

There are basically two types of handguns, revolvers and semi-automatics, and they differ significantly in design and operation.

Which type should you buy for personal protection?

Quite frequently, experienced firearm instructors recommend that newcomers to shooting choose a revolver because of comfort and simplicity of operation.

Revolvers are much easier to determine if loaded or unloaded, cocked or un-cocked and require less training when it comes to loading, unloading, handling malfunctions and cleaning. Revolvers are faster to reload than semi-autos, and offer the amateur the advantage of having fewer moving parts to master, and they are less likely to jam or misfire.

Semi-automatics are normally less bulky, they hold more ammunition and can fire more rapidly; however they require the shooter to have a greater knowledge in functional ability, loading and the unloading of the weapon, compared to a revolver. Some semi-automatic weapons are difficult to determine if they are unloaded or cocked.

While it must be a well thought-out decision as to which type of handgun you might choose, I recommend that your choice be a product of a well-respected manufacturer such as Ruger, Smith & Wesson, Glock, Colt, etc. The weapon you choose should be of sturdy construction and be able to withstand heavy use and rough handling.

Effective handgun calibers for personal protection are the .380, .38 Special, 9MM and .40 Caliber S & W. Handguns of these calibers are relatively controllable for most shooters, and they pack a significant punch, causing considerable damage to their intended target.

This should give you a pretty good idea as to choosing the right handgun, but as mentioned earlier, you should take your time and make an intelligent buying decision.

Once you have made a decision as to which weapon you prefer, it's time to consider the important legal issues. You must comply with applicable laws governing handgun ownership and use. There are a couple of forms to complete, one federal, one state and neither is too invasive in respect to your personal privacy.

You must supply details such as your name, current address, place of employment and employer's address. You are also required to provide your social security number, driver's license number, if applicable and race, sex, and place of birth.

You must be at least twenty-one years of age and never convicted of a felony or adjudged mentally incompetent by the court. To buy a handgun in South Carolina, you must be a resident of the state and be able to prove such by photo ID, and you must indicate whether or not you are presently or a past member of any subversive organizations whose agenda might be to overthrow the United States government. You must sign all forms, and by doing so, you certify that all information to be true and correct. In South Carolina, intentionally providing false information is a crime punishable as a FELONY.

The information contained on the forms is sent via telephone or computer to (NICS) National Instant Criminal Background Check System for a criminal history check by the Federal Bureau of Investigation. NICS was established as a direct result of the Brady Handgun Violence Prevention Act (Brady Act) to provide a means of checking available information to determine whether a person is disqualified from possessing a firearm under federal or state law. These records include an individual's name, sex, race, other personal descriptive data, date of birth, state of residence, and sometimes a unique identifying number.

The FBI developed the system through a joint effort with the U.S. Treasury Department, Bureau of Alcohol, Tobacco and Firearms, State and local law enforcement agencies. The NICS is a computerized background check system designed to respond within 30 seconds on most background check inquiries so licensed firearm dealers will have an almost instant answer as to the legal right of the purchaser to own a firearm. Once the NICS background check is approved, you pay for your weapon and you can be on your way. You are allowed by law to only purchase one handgun in any thirty-day period.

Incidentally, if the FBI determines that disqualifying information exists on the prospective purchaser, the Licensed Firearm Dealer will be advised that the transfer may not proceed and will be given a NICS Transaction Number to record on the ATF Form 4473.

In South Carolina it is perfectly legal to purchase a handgun from an individual who is not a licensed firearm's dealer, such as a relative, friend, fellow employee or even a total stranger, just make sure that the gun is not stolen property, and that its possession is not considered a violation of federal or state law.

Always get a signed and witnessed bill of sale from the seller, listing the sellers name, address, drivers license number (if available), and information pertinent to the gun, make, model, caliber and serial number.

Any time you purchase a gun from an individual, unless you are totally confident in the integrity of the seller and are assured that the seller knows the history of the firearm, it is a good idea to contact your local law enforcement agency, inform them of the firearm purchase and request that they run a (NCIC) National Crime Information Center records check on the gun. There should be no charge for the service, but if the gun is stolen, you will probably be visited by the police, or at least requested to deliver the gun to their headquarters. In situations involving stolen property, it's a tossup as to whether or not you will recover your money.

Losing a few dollars on a deal that turned sour is the better of the two evils. Consider the following scenario.

You purchase a gun from a fellow employee that you have been seeing at work five days a week for the last six years. The guy seems to be a really nice fellow, and you figure that you're getting a fair enough deal, the gun he's offering is worth about three-hundred dollars. You hand him one-hundred fifty dollars, get your gun, place it in the glove box of your vehicle, and go about your way, while assuming all is well.

Three months down the road you get pulled over for a routine traffic stop, and for some unexplained reason, the officer asks you if you have any firearms in your vehicle. You're an honest church going family man, with nothing to hide, so you have no reason to lie. "Yes officer, I have a .revolver in my glove box."

The officer demands to see the gun and you consent. The officer then opens the glove box and retrieves the gun, instructs you to remain seated in your vehicle as he runs the gun's serial number.

The officer returns back to your vehicle and remarks, "Sir, will you please step out of the vehicle, turnaround and face the vehicle and place both hands on top of your head." "*You are under arrest for the possession of a stolen firearm.*" You are searched, and then placed in the back seat of the officer's patrol car while he calls for a wrecker to impound your vehicle. What a nightmare, you are innocent, you didn't know that you did anything wrong. You didn't steal the gun, but now you and your attorney have the responsibility of convincing the court of your innocence. All of this could have been prevented if you had asked the authorities to run a check on the gun to start with.

Just imagine how complex that case might be if you didn't have a bill-of-sale to substantiate your purchase, and the good ol' boy at work conveniently developed a bad case of amnesia.

You are not required to have a permit to purchase a gun in South Carolina, and you do not have to register the gun with any governmental agency if purchased from an individual, however, if you purchase a gun from a licensed firearm dealer, even though technically speaking, you are not registering the gun, the record of a sale of a firearm is recorded by the U.S. Treasury Department, Bureau of Alcohol, Tobacco and Firearms.

State and federal laws also govern the sale of firearms by individuals. SECTION 16-23-30 of the South Carolina code, states that the sale or delivery of pistols and possession by certain persons is unlawful.

According to state law, it is unlawful for any person to knowingly sell, offer to sell, deliver, lease, rent, barter, exchange or transport for sale into this State any pistol to:

(1) any person who has been convicted of a crime of violence in any court of the United States, who is a fugitive from justice or a habitual drunkard or a drug addict or who has been adjudicated mentally incompetent.

(2) any person who is a member of a subversive organization.

(c) any person under the age of eighteen, (this statue shall not apply to the issuance of pistols to members of Armed Forces of the United States, active or reserve, National Guard, State Militia or R. O. T. C., when on duty or training or the temporary loan of pistols for instructions under the immediate supervision of a parent or adult instructor.)

(d) any person who by order of a circuit judge or county court judge of this State has been adjudged unfit to carry or possess a pistol, such adjudication to be made upon application by any police officer, or by any prosecuting officer of this State, or sea sponge, by the court, but any person who shall be the subject of such an application shall be entitled to reasonable notice and a proper hearing prior to any such adjudication.

The sales and purchase of firearms can be relatively simple and for the most part, an uneventful process, provided you do it in the right manner, otherwise, it could turn into a serious legal nightmare. Any time you buy or trade firearms, be smart . . . get a dated and itemized - signed receipt.

Chapter 8

Handgun Safety

The Most Important Issue!

Gun safety should never be thought of casually, it must invariably be a presence of mind that consciously and subconsciously directs your behavior whenever you use, carry or store a firearm.

HANDGUN SAFETY - The Most Important Issue!

Safety must be your *NUMBER ONE* concern anytime you are handling or using a firearm of any type. You must treat your firearm with extreme caution whether you're at home, target shooting or carrying a legally concealed weapon. Any firearm must be treated with respect, even if you know it to be unloaded at the time.

The majority of firearm accidents occur through *carelessness* and *ignorance*. Carelessness is defined as *inattentive* or *marked by or resulting from lack of thought*. This book can provide you with the knowledge to enable you to act safely while dealing with firearms and self-defense matters, but it is your duty to implement what you learn to become a responsible gun owner, and you must try diligently to refrain from developing bad habits and careless actions.

I cannot do much about carelessness on your part, other than to warn you of the consequences that often occur when the two come together; carelessness and firearms. Tragedy!

Ignorance relating to firearms is a subject that we can deal with effectively. The dictionary defines ignorance as *being without education or knowledge*, by the time you finish this chapter, hopefully you will be knowledgeable in firearm safety and the need for it at all times.

Firearm safety must become second nature to the extent that it will cause you to literally cringe if you see someone with a firearm act contrary to what you have learned about firearm safety. When knowledgeable people exercise responsible firearm ownership, accidents will not happen.

Firearm accidents are generally 100 per-cent avoidable. By learning and applying safety rules for proper firearms handling and storage, no one need ever experience the pain and agony that result from firearm accidents. Learning and applying the basic rules of proper firearm handling can help you avoid unnecessary mishaps.

FOUR CARDINAL RULES OF FIREARM SAFETY -

* Treat <u>all</u> firearms as if they are loaded.

* Always keep the muzzle pointed in a safe direction.

* Keep your finger off the trigger until you are ready to fire.

* Know your target and what is beyond it.

SAFETY RULE NUMBER 1 - Treat <u>all</u> firearms as if they are loaded.

Any guns that you do not use for your immediate personal protection should be stored unloaded, separated from ammunition and in a secured place that is not accessible to children and unauthorized users. The guns should be stored in a lock box or gun safe.

"*I didn't have any idea that the gun was loaded*!" These tragic words are often uttered after a friend or a family member has committed a gun accident. You should NEVER decrease the amount of respect for your gun, even if you know that it is not loaded. All guns should be treated as if they were loaded.

Here is why this is important. You could be wrong and the gun actually be loaded. It may have just slipped your mind, and you forgot to unload it as you normally do. <u>No bullet fired deliberately or accidentally, can be stopped</u>. You were in a hurry, and you may have left a cartridge in the chamber. Innocent mistakes do happen. *Don't take the chance; all guns should be treated as if they are loaded.*

Unsafe gun handling practices are a bad habit. If you get into the habit of handling an *empty gun* carelessly, as a result of human nature, you probably will unconsciously, through habit, display the same bad habit in the handling of a loaded gun. The results of the bad habit could prove disastrous.

SAFETY RULE NUMBER 2 - Keep the muzzle pointed in a safe direction.

Your gun must always be pointed in a safe direction. Although circumstances somewhat dictate what is considered a safe direction, normally, that direction would be down toward the ground. If you are on the top floor of a two-story building, and people are in the area below, down would not be considered the safe direction, you probably would be wise to hold your gun with the barrel pointing upwards toward the sky.

This would be a judgment decision, and you must exercise your common sense to make the right decision. Abiding by this important safety rule puts the odds in your favor that you would not accidentally injure or kill someone if your gun accidentally discharges.

SAFETY RULE NUMBER 3 Keep your finger off the trigger until you are ready to fire.

Even though human instinct is to place your finger on the trigger when holding a gun, the sole purpose of the trigger is for firing the gun; it is not designed as a resting place for your forefinger. You can rest your finger along the side the handgun, on the trigger guard.

When you are ready to fire, whether arising out of need of a self-defense situation, or out target shooting on the firing range, moving your finger from the "index rest position" to "active fire position" will only take a millisecond or so.

If your finger is constantly resting on the trigger in the "active-fire position," it is much too easy to slip-up and fire the gun accidentally. You could stumble and fall, even a sudden loud noise could startle you, either might cause you to accidentally squeeze the trigger and fire the gun.

Even experienced shooters are subject to the same involuntary human reflex which can cause you to jerk or cause your muscles to become tense causing a trigger pull. *Keep your finger of the trigger!*

This rule applies whether you are target shooting with a handgun, hunting quail with a shotgun, or deer hunting with your favorite high-powered rifle, the consequences of carelessness can result in either situation. Even law enforcement agencies train their officers to "*keep their fingers off the trigger until they are ready to shoot.*"

Accidents do happen. I am familiar with an incident where two Sheriffs' Deputies were responding to a call, where there had been a shooting incident reported and the dispatcher warned the deputies of the possible danger. Both deputies speculating that the aggressor might be around the next corner carried their .38 caliber weapons drawn and ready for business.

Well, here is where the situation went from bad to worse. As the deputies went around the corner of the house into the back yard, they realized that the aggressor had apparently crawled over a barbed wire fence in his flee to freedom. The lead deputy managed to clear the fence and as the second deputy approached the fence, his .38 caliber revolver still in hand . . . ***POW!*** . . . The deputy in front was wounded as the bullet grazed his head.

The second deputy had stumbled and with his finger on the trigger, fired an accidental shot hitting his partner. With almost surgical precision, the single bullet from the second deputy's revolver removed most of the first deputies left ear. The injury was serious, and if the shot had been an inch or so to the wrong direction, it could have been a fatal shot.

This was clearly an accident and could have been prevented. The accident was an act of carelessness, and if the deputy's finger had not been on the trigger, the accident would not have happened.

SAFETY RULE NUMBER 4 - Be sure of your target and what is beyond it.

You should always know your target and what is behind it. You are civilly and criminally responsible for any damages that might occur from the instant that your bullet leaves the muzzle of your firearm, until which time it comes to a complete stop. In other words, if you fire your handgun carelessly into an area that is not secure, and as a result of your firing the gun someone is injured or killed by your bullet, you will be criminally charged.

In the same scenario, if your bullet strikes a home, an automobile or other personal property, you may be subject to civil litigation, and if found liable, it could cost you a considerable amount of money. If you're not sure of what your bullet will be hitting when fired, or where it will ultimately end, don't pull the trigger.

With today's high-powered ammunition, your bullet may pass through your target and hit a person or valuable object. You must always use extreme caution when firing at or near hard or flat objects, water included. Your bullet can ricochet and the results of such can be serious.

A safety-minded hunter always acquires a good target before pulling the trigger, he actually sees the deer, turkey or other game in his sights, and knows that the area behind the game is clear before ever firing a shot. A stirring in the bushes is not sufficient for the responsible hunter, he will not fire until he visually identifies his target, the stirring could be a fellow hunter, or even a couple of kids playing hide-and-go-seek.

The same practice should apply to that of a person carrying a handgun for personal protection. Knowing what is beyond your target is absolutely necessary, whether you are target practicing, or you are actually involved in a self-defense situation. Always know your target and what is behind it.

OTHER SAFETY ISSUES - Never point a gun at anything that you are unwilling to destroy.

There are many things that you value and don't want to damage or destroy by putting a bullet hole in it, for example, walls, doors, home and office furnishings, automobiles, or even your dog or cat, but far more significant, a human being. Under no circumstances, should you ever playfully aim any firearm at any human being. NEVER point your firearm in the direction of people.

NEVER point a firearm at objects that people may be in or behind.

Most people get disturbed if someone randomly points a firearm at them or for that matter, anyone else. Informing someone about proper firearm etiquette or even abruptly intervening is justified as circumstances warrant.
In South Carolina, the act of pointing a firearm at another person is a criminal offense.

SECTION 16-23-410. Pointing a firearm at any person.

It is unlawful for a person to present or point at another person a loaded or unloaded firearm. A person who violates the provisions of this section is guilty of a felony and, upon conviction, must be fined in the discretion of the court or imprisoned not more than five years. This section must not be construed to abridge the right of self-defense or to apply to theatricals or like performances.

There are several risks to consider in playfully pointing a firearm at another person. You risk accidentally injuring or causing the death of the person that you are pointing the firearm. You risk being criminally charged, as provided by state law, and you can be charged and convicted even if the gun is not loaded. And finally, the person that you are pointing the gun at might fail to see the humor in your actions, and if they have a weapon available, might act in self defense, and according to state law, the action would be justified. Obviously, SECTION 16-23-410 does not restrict your right in pointing a gun at an assailant, if you are acting in self-defense.

OTHER SAFETY ISSUES - Keep your gun at its minimum level of readiness.

As discussed earlier in Safety Rule Number 3, any guns that you do not use for personal protection should be stored unloaded in a secured place that is not accessible to unauthorized users. That means exactly what it says, however, it is my suggestion and nothing more, that you keep the gun that you use for personal protection, available and loaded. You must keep that gun in a secured location, even if under your bed in a locked box.

There are pros and cons regarding this matter. Some firearm safety organizations consider it unsafe to have a gun that close to your bedside. The important fact to consider is, would you be cognizant enough to safely and intelligently handle a life or death situation?

If you were awakened from a deep sleep, would you be able to make the proper decision? Would you jump-up and start squeezing the trigger, or could you carefully and rationally analyze the situation to determine exactly what was happening before taking any offensive actions? Would you be rational enough to distinguish between right and wrong, good or bad, that difference could be the difference between life and death of a family member?

Personally, I keep my .40 caliber Glock loaded and within arms reach. If I am awakened during the night by a intruder, the last thing I want to have to do is go scrambling around the house looking for my handgun and ammo, however, come morning, my ritual is to place the gun in a safe area.

This matter is of a very serious and personal nature, and only you are capable of knowing what is right for you. Personally, I know what I am capable of doing should an emergency situation arise, and I can train you to act accordingly, but what you may do under a so-called dream state is something that I am not qualified to deal with.

OTHER SAFETY ISSUES - Use only the correct ammunition.

Incorrect ammunition can cause all kinds of malfunctions, and some may prove to be fatal. Just because the ammunition may fit in your gun does not mean that it is the proper ammo for that gun. Extra powder ammo ("+P" or "+P+") could possibly cause the gun to blow up in your hand, and you can imagine the seriousness of an injury it might cause. Ammo that is too small in caliber for the gun can slide into and lodge in the gun's barrel, if this happens, a correct round is loaded and fired, the obstructed barrel could actually explode in the hand of the shooter. Always use extreme caution in selecting the ammo for your gun. The correct type of ammo is most always printed on the side of the gun.

ALWAYS WEAR EYE AND EAR PROTECTION

The sound from a gunshot is loud, and the constant exposure of such sound can cause damage to your hearing. Firing a couple of shots every now and then without ear protection shouldn't give you any long lasting ear problems, however, hearing damage is cumulative, and that means frequent exposure to the loud sound from gunfire without ear protection, will eventually cause nerve damage and maybe even deafness.

The firing of handguns produces debris and gases which can be damaging to your eyes. Semi-automatic pistols automatically eject fired cases which can easily expend powder debris into your eyes, and there is always the risk of the ejected casing popping back and hitting you in one eye or the other.

Due to the possibilities of injury to the eyes and ears, you should always wear proper eye and ear protection. For target shooting, it is important to wear protection (glasses) that have protective side pieces. It is always a good idea for the shooter to wear a hat with a brim that comes down over the top of the protective glasses to block any airborne shell cases that might try to pop in from the top of the glasses.

Hearing protection is available in a couple of different types. There is the Ear Muff headphone type with the band that straps over the shooter's head, and there is the ear plug type, which actually fits into the shooter's ears. The headphone type ear device offers the most protection, and is normally required at indoor shooting ranges.

The reason for that is the sound pressure from an exploding cartridge has a limited area to dissipate and as a result, sound waves bounce back from the walls to the shooter. This damaging pressure can be transferred by the temporal bone of the human skull, which is situated behind the ear, to the inner ear, eventually causing considerable damage to the nerves of the inner ear, and the shooter may not even be aware that it is happening.

I realize that in the event of a self-defense situation you don't need to waste time putting on your eye and ear protection, and I don't think you will be confronted by an aggressor that will be considerate enough to allow you the time to put your eye and ear protection in place, However, you're out shooting at cola cans or targets, it is a good idea to make use of your eye and ear protection.

ALCOHOL, DRUGS AND FIREARMS. . . <u>A deadly trio</u>!

A mixed drink, beer or wine as well as any other substance (drug) has a tendency of impairing normal mental behavior and slowing down the ordinary physical functions of the human body to an extent that the possession of a firearm is considered a significant safety risk to the person and a threat to any person in his immediate area.

That one sentence alone should be meaningful enough to persuade any intelligent person to stay away from a firearm of any type while that person is consuming alcohol, using drugs, or even taking some medications. This applies to some over the counter medication, as well as some medication which has been prescribed by a physician.

Those substances, alcohol and drugs can cause a person to be severely judgment impaired and/or suffer from undesirable physical side effects such as vision difficulties, loss of coordination, drowsiness or others symptoms, any of which might contribute to an accident involving the firearm. Firearms should not be carried or handled by a person under the influence of alcohol or drugs.

YOUR GUN'S SAFETY DEVICE -

Your gun's safety, if so equipped, is a mechanical device normally found on semi-automatic handguns, and if properly engaged, will prevent the gun from firing. The purpose of the safety is to prevent the accidental firing of the gun.

The safety devices on most rifles and shotguns are *not drop proof* safety devices, they simply block the trigger. For a gun's safety to be *drop proof,* the safety mechanism must block the firing pin or the hammer.

A safety is a mechanical device and any mechanical device can fail!

Never totally rely on your gun's safety, use it but don't bet your life or the life of someone else on it. Always keep in mind that even the best safety device is not as safe as an unloaded gun. Never just pull the trigger of your firearm just because you think the safety is on, even if you think it is unloaded. Always visually and physically inspect your firearm to be absolutely sure that it is unloaded, and always point the firearm downrange, or in another safe direction before you pull the trigger.

You should never relax your safe handling practices just because you think a gun is unloaded, no more than you should be any less careful with a loaded gun just because you know that the safety is on.

A WELL-CARED FOR FIREARM IS A SAFE FIREARM

A firearm is a precision instrument, and with any precision instrument, it is essential that it be given proper care in order for it to operate correctly and *safely*. That care will extend the usable life of the firearm and help maintain its value.

There are several safety factors which must be considered when cleaning a firearm; however, the most important is that you always treat your firearm as if it were loaded. If you are consistent in observing that safety rule, you will find these gun cleaning safety rules to be simple.

SAFETY TIP: Make sure the gun is empty (check cylinder, magazine removed and check chamber).

SAFETY TIP: The chamber is swung open (revolver)**, or the slide is locked back** (semi-automatic).

SAFETY TIP: Be certain that no ammunition is present in the area where you are cleaning your firearm.

<u>**ALWAYS REMEMBER:**</u>

You cannot readily determine whether or not a handgun is loaded simply by looking at it. You need to know how each type of handgun operates in order to exercise proper gun safety.

Chapter 9

HANDGUNS

Types and Parts

A Handgun is a weapon consisting essentially of a metal tube from which a bullet is fired.

Handguns or pistols, as they are also known, began to develop popularity somewhere around the first-half of the 16th century, when the *wheel lock,* the first practical mechanical ignition device was invented. Early handguns were much too heavy and awkward to be carried in a side holster as a weapon of self-defense.

Today the handgun is the weapon of choice for self-defense, and in the United States alone there are more than 75 million handguns in circulation.

A handgun is a precision built mechanical instrument. For proper and safe operation, full knowledge of how it works is essential. In this chapter you will learn about the various types of handguns and their intricate workings. You will become familiar with parts of the handgun and learn exactly what function each part plays in its overall operation.

TYPES OF HANDGUNS

The two most frequently used handguns in today's society are the revolver and the semi-automatic, and each share three of the same major component characteristics, *frame*, *barrel*, and *action*. Although the two types of handguns have components that are somewhat similar in design, their workings are considerably different.

THE REVOLVER

In order to fully understand the operation of a revolver and learn how to safely use it, you must be familiar with its individual parts and know exactly what each part does. The revolver is equipped with a cylinder that consists of several chambers, normally five or six, those individual chambers are used for holding cartridges (bullets) in position while waiting to be fired. As the revolver's trigger is pulled, the cylinder rotates and stops, precisely placing the next chamber in line between the firing pin and the barrel, then instantaneously the cartridge is fired.

There are two types of revolvers. The most popular and widely used is the double-action revolver, and its name is derived from the fact that the trigger performs two distinct tasks, or *two actions*. On the double-action revolver, when the trigger is pulled, the hammer engages and releases, thus striking the firing pin and firing the cartridge. However, with a single-action revolver, the hammer has to be manually engaged, pulled-back by the shooter and remain engaged until the revolver is fired or the trigger is safely released by the shooter.

Pulling the trigger will not engage the hammer on a single-action revolver, as its name implies, the trigger performs only one single task, and that is to release the previously engaged hammer so that it will strike the firing pin, subsequently firing the cartridge in line to be fired

.

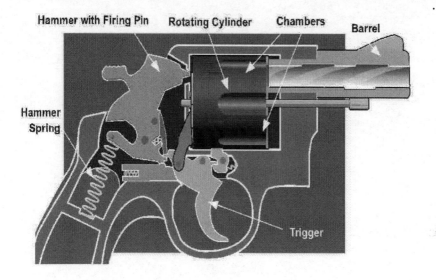

THE PARTS OF THE REVOLVER

The <u>frame</u> is the backbone of any firearm, whether it's a rifle, shotgun or a handgun, but being more specific in this topic, the *frame* is the backbone of the revolver, and is the major component to which all other parts are attached.

The <u>grips</u>, also known as grip panels, are attached by machine screws to each side of the frames lower part, the back-strap, sometimes called the butt. Grips are normally made of wood, plastic, rubber, and occasionally bone.

The <u>back-strap</u> is the rear of the frame; it is an integral part of the frame itself, and not a separately attached component. The back-strap is the metal piece that is located, (sandwiched) between the two grips.

The <u>trigger guard</u> is located on the underside of the revolver's frame. In most all revolvers, the trigger guard is a part of the frame and its only purpose is to protect the trigger from being accidentally pulled, however, it makes a convenient place to rest the trigger finger prior to the firing of the revolver. Hence, always keep your finger off the trigger until you are ready to fire.

The <u>rear sight</u> is located on top of the frame and is the sighting device closest to the hammer. Normally, the front and rear sights are part of the frame, however, on some firearms the rear sights are separately attached components attached to the frame and are adjustable for firing accuracy.

The <u>front sight</u> is an integral part of the barrel and is located at the end of the barrel where the bullet leaves the muzzle. The front and rear sites are used in conjunction for the accurate aiming of the firearm.

The <u>barrel</u> is the cylindrical metallic shaft of a firearm through which the bullet travels after being fired.

The <u>bore</u> is the inside of the barrel. It is not a separate part attached to the barrel; it is a precisely machined opening within the barrel in which the projectile/bullet passes after being fired.

The bore has spiral cuts which have been precision milled by the handgun manufacturer, and run from one end of the barrel to the other. These cuts are called <u>grooves</u>. The metal ridges in between each groove are called lands. The combination of the two is referred to as <u>rifling</u>.

Measuring the distance of the lands (one side of the bore to the other) determines the caliber of the firearm.

The measurement is calculated in hundredths of an inch, or in millimeters, resulting in calibers such as .22, .38, .40 and so on, or in the case of millimeters, there are 9mm, 10mm and a few others.

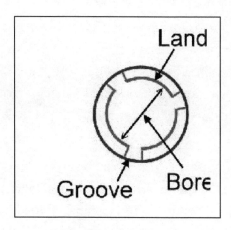

The purpose of the rifling is to cause the fired projectile/bullet to spin as it travels through the barrel, and the continual spinning effect of the bullet aids in its stability and accuracy on the way to its target.

The <u>muzzle</u> is the front end of the barrel where the bullet exits after being fired.

The <u>action</u> as the name implies, is a combination of moving parts used to load, fire and unload a handgun and attached to the frame.

The <u>trigger</u> is located on the underside of the handgun, surrounded by the trigger guard and is a moving part connected to the frame. The triggers' main function is to activate or cock the hammer, which in turn strikes the firing pin and fires the cartridge.

The <u>hammer</u> is located at the top rear and is a moving part attached to the frame. The purpose of the hammer after being activated by the trigger is to strike the firing pin.

The <u>hammer spur</u> is the flat surface of the hammer and is ridged or grooved so that the shooter's thumb has a better grip in engaging the hammer.

The <u>firing pin</u> is attached to the hammer on some handguns; on others it is located inside the frame. The only purpose of the firing pin is to strike cartridges' primer causing it to ignite, thus firing the cartridge.

As previously mentioned, the <u>cylinder</u> consists of several chambers (normally five or six); those chambers are arranged in a round pattern and are used for holding cartridges in place within the handgun's cylinder. A chamber is a precisely machined tubular shaped opening that is used for holding cartridges in place, while waiting to be fired.

The <u>cylinder release latch</u> is a part on many revolvers and is attached to the frame. The function of the release latch is to allow the handgun's cylinder to swing-out for loading, unloading and cleaning. Some "old type" revolvers without cylinder release latches provide a machine bolt that holds the cylinder in place, which can be unscrewed and temporarily removed. This allows the cylinder to "dropout" for loading, and the process reversed for placing the handgun back in firing order.

The <u>ejector</u> or <u>extractor</u> is attached to the ejector rod which is also the cylinder axle. The function of these moving parts is to aid in the removal of ammunition or fired cases from the handgun's cylinder.

THE SEMI-AUTOMATIC

The physical components and fundamental operating procedures of a semi-automatic handgun are substantially different from that of a revolver. Cartridges otherwise known as ammunition, is placed in a storage device called the magazine or clip and inserted into the magazine port of the handgun. Magazines have a storage capacity of as few as six, to as many as fifteen or more cartridges.

The shooter initially has to manually retract the semi-automatics' slide, and as the slide returns to its normally closed position, the first cartridge is cycled into the chamber. During this motion the hammer automatically activates and is standing-by for the action from the trigger. With the revolver, when the shooter pulls the trigger, the hammer closes striking the firing pin, thus firing the cartridge.

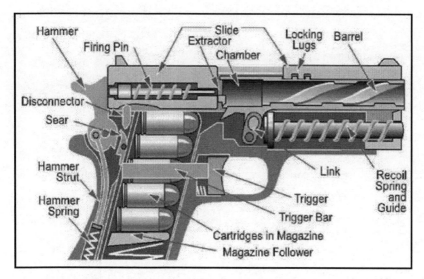

From then, until all cartridges which are stored in the magazine have been fired, the shooter can simply pull the trigger each time he chooses to fire a cartridge, hence, the term semi-automatic is derived. Once the magazine is empty, the shooter must remove the magazine from the handgun, and reload.

The cycle continues, as discussed in the previous paragraph, as long as the shooter chooses to shoot. As previously stated, the operating procedures of a semi-automatic are different from that of a revolver; however, both type handguns have the same three major components, the *frame*, the *barrel* and the *action*. The <u>frame</u>, as with the revolver, is the backbone of the semi-automatic to which all component parts are attached.

The semi-automatic has a feature that revolvers normally do not have, and that is a safety. The safety is a mechanical device when activated reduces the chances of an accidental discharging of a cartridge. The safety device is further discussed in the *"Handgun Safety"* chapter of this book.

The <u>slide lock,</u> also known as slide release is a device that locks the slide in the rear position. The slide lock engages when the last cartridge is fired leaving the chamber port open. This action informs the shooter that the firearm's magazine and chamber are free of ammunition. At any time, the slide can be manually retracted and the slide lock engaged to provide visual inspection of the firearm.

This can be done with or without ammunition being present in the magazine or chamber, but always use caution if the magazine or the chamber has live cartridges. When the slide lock is released and the slide returns to normal position the firearm will be armed and ready to fire. Even if you know the handgun is empty, you must still treat it as if it is loaded.

The recoil spring forces the slide to return to its closed position any time that a new cartridge is retrieved from the magazine, or when the shooter has manually opened the slide and released it.

The de-cocking lever is another lever which is attached to the frame of some semi-automatics, and can be somewhat considered as a safety device. This lever allows the shooter to *safely* lower the "cocked" hammer to the resting position. The device actually engages a metal shield between the hammer and the firing pin to prevent an accidental discharge. The de-cocking procedure for a semi-automatic pistol can vary greatly from model to model.

The grips, also known as the grip panels, are attached by machine screws to each side of the frames lower section, sometimes called the butt. Grips are normally made of wood, plastic, rubber, and occasionally, bone.

The back-strap, again like the revolver, is the rear of the frame; it is an integral part of the frame and is not a separate device. The back-strap is the metal piece that is sandwiched in between the two grips.

The trigger guard is located on the underside of the revolver's frame. As with the revolver, the trigger guard is an integral part of the frame and its sole purpose is to protect the trigger from being accidentally pulled and discharging a cartridge.

Remember - always keep your finger off the trigger until you are ready to fire.

The barrel is the cylindrical metallic shaft of a firearm through which the bullet travels after being fired. The barrel of the semi-automatic is similar to that of the revolver, with one significant difference; the rear of the barrel of the semi-automatic has one chamber, compared to five or six chambers of the revolver.

The muzzle is the front end of the barrel where the bullet exits after being fired. The bore is the inside of the barrel. As with the revolver, it is not a separate part attached to the barrel, it is the precisely machined opening within the barrel in which the projectile/bullet passes after being fired.

The bore has spiral cuts which have been precision milled by the handgun manufacturer, and run from one end of the barrel to the other. These cuts are called grooves. The metal ridges in between each groove are called lands. The combination of the two is referred to as rifling.

The action is the combination of moving parts used to load, fire and unload the semi-automatic handgun, and the parts are attached to the frame. There are vast number of mechanical designs and configurations for that of a semi-automatic handgun, and the actions of the various types can vary significantly.

Some semi-automatic handguns have external hammers; some have internal hammers which are integral working parts of the internal firing mechanism.

The internal firing mechanism is actually inside of the handgun and generally cannot be seen without being disassembled. The internal firing mechanism is the device that strikes the firing pin, which strikes the cartridge's primer, causing it to fire. Handguns of this nature are frequently referred to as "hammerless."

The slide is a common element in all semi-automatic handguns. The slide arrangement can vary in different makes and models of semi-automatic handguns, in some makes, the slide encases the entire barrel, in others, and it is located to the rear of the firearm.

The purpose of the slide is to cycle a cartridge from the magazine to the firing chamber, empty the fired casing, and then again cycle another cartridge from the magazine to the firing chamber. This slide function will take place with every cartridge fired.

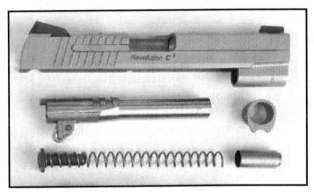

The front and rear sights are normally located on the top front and rear of the slide, although in some models the sights may be a part of the barrel or the frame. Sites are used for the accurate aiming.

The hammer, if so equipped, is located at the top rear and is a moving part attached to the frame. After being engaged, the trigger activates the hammer, causing it to strike the firing pin.

The hammer spur, if so equipped, is the flat surface of the hammer and is ridged or grooved so that the shooter's thumb has a better grip in engaging the hammer.

The magazine or clip is the semi-automatics' cartridge storage device and keeps cartridges ready to be cycled into the chamber by the slide. The cartridges held in the magazine are forced upward by the tension of the magazine spring causing any available cartridge directly in the path of the slide to be individually placed into the chamber for firing as the need arises.

The <u>magazine release</u> is a button or lever which releases the magazine from the handgun's magazine port.

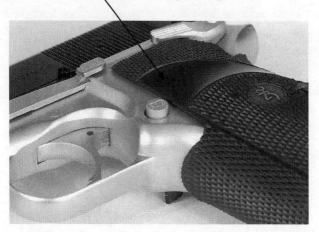

The <u>trigger</u> is located on the underside of the handgun, surrounded by the trigger guard and is a moving part connected to the frame. The trigger's main function is to activate or cock the hammer or internal firing mechanism, which in turn strikes the firing pin and fires the cartridge.

The <u>single-action</u>, the <u>double-action</u> and the <u>double-action only</u> makes up the three different kinds of semi-automatic handguns. As the revolver, the action of the semi-automatics trigger determines the operation of the handgun.

The <u>single-action</u> semi-automatics' trigger performs a single function; it releases the hammer causing the firing pin to strike the cartridge. If the shooter fails to manually engage the hammer and pulls the trigger, nothing will happen.

The <u>double-action</u> semi-automatics' trigger performs two functions; it "cocks" the hammer or internal firing mechanism and releases it. This action causes the firing pin to strike and fire a cartridge if one is in the chamber, the slide will automatically eject the casing and reload the chamber with a new cartridge, thus engaging the hammer for additional firing.

If there is no cartridge present in the chamber, it simply "dry fires," the slide does not retract and a new cartridge is not loaded into the chamber. *** Dry firing a handgun is never recommended**.

With a <u>double-action</u> semi-automatic, the action will also function as a single-action, if there is a live cartridge present in the chamber, for the first shot, the shooter can simply pull the hammer back with his thumb and lightly pull the trigger and the handgun will fire. After the first cartridge fires, the hammer will remain engaged.

The <u>double-action only</u> semi-automatic is designed in such a way that the trigger will engage and release the hammer on the first and all successive shots, provided that there is a live cartridge present in the chamber for the first shot. The slide will chamber a new cartridge after each shot, however, unlike the standard double-action, the hammer will not remain cocked after each shot. To fire another shot, the shooter must squeeze the trigger, which cocks and releases the hammer, as with the first shot.

The major difference between the double-action semi-automatic and the double-action only semi-automatic is that when the double-action semi-automatic fires, the slide ejects the casing, reloads a new cartridge and the hammer remains engaged for additional firing. If there are no additional shots to be fired, the shooter must engage the decoking lever to drop the hammer to its safe position.

With the double-action only semi-automatic, when the shooter fires a cartridge, the slide ejects and reloads the chamber, but the hammer does not remain cocked, however, the shooter simply needs to pull the trigger to fire another cartridge.

Even though the general operating procedure of one revolver is generally about the same for another, please take special caution when dealing with semi-automatics. The descriptions in this chapter were only that of a couple makes and there are innumerable mechanical designs for semi-automatic handguns.

Always read the manufacturers instruction manual for a particular handgun very carefully, and be sure that you fully understand the operating procedures for the firearm you are using. If you do not <u>fully</u> understand a particular firearm's operation, <u>put it down until you can get some knowledgeable help</u>. The risk is too great!

SAFETY TIP: You need to know how each type of handgun operates in order to exercise proper gun safety.

Chapter 10

HANDGUN OPERATION

The skills of loading, preparing to shoot, and unloading handguns are all basic skills which every shooter must master.

The first step in making a handgun ready to fire is to load it. Revolvers and semi-automatic arc loaded differently; however, if you are familiar with the procedure, loading either is a simple task.

DOUBLE-ACTION REVOLVERS

Loading a revolver

Keeping the handgun pointed in a safe direction and your finger off the trigger, hold the handgun in the left hand with the muzzle pointed in a safe direction. (Instruction for right-handed shooters.)

Push the cylinder release latch forward with the thumb of the right hand, while pushing the cylinder open with the two-middle fingers of the left hand. This will allow the cylinder to swing open for loading. Never open the cylinder forcefully, this careless action could damage the cylinder's alignment, and prove costly to repair.

Continuing to hold the handgun in the left hand, load the required number of cartridges into the handgun's cylinder with the right hand. After loading is complete, return the cylinder to its closed position with the thumb of the left hand.

Most modern double-action revolvers can be safely holstered and carried with a live round in the chamber directly under the firing pin. Older single-action and western-style revolvers cannot, due to the fact that the handgun's firing pin actually rests on the cartridge's primer or rim.

Ordinarily, revolvers do not have safety devices, thus, when the handgun is loaded, it is ready to fire. If you choose to fire the revolver double-action, after being absolutely sure of your target and what is beyond, gently pull the trigger for each shot you choose to fire.

If you choose to fire the revolver as a single-action revolver, while gripping the handgun with the right hand, use the left thumb to pull the handguns hammer back until it reaches its locked position. The handgun is now ready to fire as a single-action revolver.

Firing the revolver single-action will allow the shooter an easier trigger pull since the mechanics of the handgun will only have to perform one task, which is the releasing of the hammer, rather than cocking and releasing, as in double-action. The shooter will have to perform the same task each time he or she chooses to fire the revolver in single-action style.

Normally, revolvers do not have de-cocking levers as do some semi-automatics; therefore, the shooter must learn the technique of how to safely de-cock the hammer of the revolver. Remember to always keep the handgun pointed in a safe direction and the finger off of the trigger.

Since the hammer is already in a cocked position, the shooter should place the left thumb in the space in between the handgun's firing pin and the hammer. This will serve as a buffer or safety to prevent the hammer from accidentally striking the firing pin.

Now place your right thumb securely onto the cocked hammer's spur while safely controlling the action or movement of the hammer. Carefully remove your left thumb from its safety duty while gently squeezing the trigger. You will feel the hammer's action unlock, and this will permit you to slowly allow it to return to the un-cocked position. Learning to safely de cock a revolver is easy and can be mastered with only a little practice.

To unload the revolver, hold the handgun pointed in a safe direction and your finger off the trigger. Hold the handgun in the left hand with the muzzle pointed downward.

Push the cylinder release latch forward with the thumb of the right hand while pushing the cylinder open with the two-middle fingers of the left hand. This will allow the cylinder to swing open for unloading. As previously mentioned, never open the cylinder forcefully, or cause it to slam shut, this careless action may damage the cylinder's alignment and prove to be very costly.

While holding the handgun with the left hand, raise the level of the muzzle to a position higher than the cylinder. Use the left thumb to push the handgun's ejector rod causing any unfired cartridges or empty cases to be pushed out of the cylinder.

Use the right hand to catch the ejected cartridges or empty cases. After the task of unloading is complete, with the thumb of the left hand, return the cylinder to its normal closed position. The handgun is safely unloaded for storage.

While shooting, if only a couple of cartridges have been fired, and you choose to reload the revolver to full-capacity(topped-off), open the handgun's cylinder and engage(push) the extractor rod half-way. This will allow the shooter to replace the fired rounds (empty cases) with live ammunition. When this procedure is completed, return the cylinder to its closed position.

SEMI-AUTOMATIC

Loading and unloading the semi-automatic is significantly different from that of a revolver and requires an entirely different procedure. With the revolver, the shooter should always keep the handgun pointed in a safe direction and finger off the trigger.

Hold the handgun in the right hand with the muzzle pointed downward. If the handgun's magazine (clip) has not previously been removed, do so by engaging the magazine release with the left thumb.

With the left hand, retract the handgun's slide to the open and locked position and carefully inspect the handgun's chamber, being completely positive that there are no live cartridges in the chamber.

To load the semi-automatic handgun, once you are absolutely sure that the weapon is unloaded, you may temporarily lay it down in a safe location. Refer to your handgun owner's manual and be absolutely sure as to the number of cartridges your handgun's magazine is designed to hold. (Do not try to place more cartridges in the magazine than it is designed to safely handle.)

After being sure that you have the correct ammunition for your handgun, load the required number of cartridges into the magazine by pushing the cartridges into and down toward the rear of the magazine. Repeat this process until you have loaded the desired number of cartridges.

When you have finished loading the magazine, pickup the handgun and place it securely in the right hand. Using the left hand, replace the magazine back into the handgun, making sure that you are inserting the cartridges facing the correct direction. The magazine will only fit properly in one position, do not try to force it, this may damage the magazine and handgun.

Release the slide stop with the left thumb, allowing the slide to move to its closed position. This action automatically strips off the magazine's top cartridge and places it into the handgun's chamber. When releasing the slide, do not try to "hold it back" or to guide it to the forward position, allow it to snap or spring in place under its own power. This action is necessary for proper operation and the cycling of live ammunition. As jolting as it may seem, the semi-automatic handgun will not be damaged if you allow the slide to act as it was designed. Your handgun is now loaded and ready to fire.

Some handgun's safety device will automatically engage upon loading or reloading, but that is not true in all cases.

If you are not going to fire the handgun immediately, be sure that the safety device is set, always keep the handgun pointed in a safe direction and your finger off the trigger until you are ready to fire.

If you have fired all cartridges which were loaded into the magazine, your weapon is now empty and the semi-automatic does not retain empty cases. If you have not fired all of the cartridges, the following guideline will assist you in safely unloading the weapon.

When unloading a semi-automatic pistol, with it pointed in a safe direction and the trigger finger being outside the trigger guard, the proper sequence is: (1) Remove the magazine; (2) rack the action several times to clear the chamber; (3) lock the slide open and (4) visually and physically inspect the chamber and magazine well. When you are positive that the gun is empty, release the slide and allow it to return to the closed position by activating the slide release.

You should now empty the cartridges from the loaded magazine, replace them in the cartridge container and place the magazine back into the handgun's magazine port.

Unlike revolvers, due to the vast number of designs and mechanical operations, all semi-automatics do not operate the same. The method of un-cocking varies as to make and model; therefore I cannot safely or effectively cover that issue without risking the omission of important information.

If you have a semi-automatic handgun and you are not absolutely sure of its proper operation, please seek professional advice from a licensed gun dealer or other qualified individual. Don't take a chance.

Loading and unloading a handgun, whether a revolver or semi-automatic is a simple task and can be easily mastered. You must be totally familiar with your handguns operation before you can safely manage it; that part it is up to you.

Practice makes perfect, and for you to be able to adequately master this precision mechanical device you must practice.

SAFETY TIP:

When firing a handgun if a cartridge fails to fire, immediately point the weapon in a safe direction, and as a precaution in the event of a hang fire, wait at least 30 seconds, open the action and remove the cartridge.

Chapter 11

AMMUNITION

Common sense will tell you when the ammunition is more powerful, greater stopping power is possible, and stopping power is a major consideration when it comes to self-defense. However, there are two significant factors that should be considered, and they must be carefully considered in your choice of a self-defense weapon.

To increase the power exerted from the cartridge, it is necessary to increase the size of the cartridge in order to contain a larger amount of gun powder and a larger bullet. The size of a handgun will vary according to caliber. The higher the caliber of ammunition, the larger the handgun's physical size must be. This is necessary for safety and for the requirement of ammunition capacity. Second, and equally important, more powerful handguns are considerably more difficult to control, especially for a beginner or person of small stature.

Not only are there numerous caliber cartridges, which the list is too long to provide, there are also many different styles of cartridges. Round nose, hollow point, truncated cone, wad cutter, semi-wad cutters and a few others, and the distinguishing difference is in the shape of the bullet.

The hollow point has been determined to be the most suitable cartridge for self-defense. The hollow point cartridge contains a cavity in the front of the bullet that allows the lead bullet to expand on contact with body tissue or fluids. This expansion of the bullet on impact causes considerably more knockdown force, and prevents the over penetration of your target. In the event of self-defense, your bullet should affect only your intended target, and should not pass-on through you target and hit an innocent victim.

Ammunition manufacturers in an effort to provide quality ammunition capable of reliable man-stopping power have created many variations of the hollow point design. In addition to the increased stopping power, this ammunition is less likely to penetrate walls, making them the choice for apartment dwellers. The downside to ammunition is that some find to be extraordinarily loud.

These types of ammunition are certainly suitable choices for self-defense, but considering their high cost, you might be just as well served by a conventional hollow point design. There are two different types of cartridges made for use in today's modern handguns, the center fire and the rim-fire. On the previous page we described the components of the center-fire cartridge.

The rim-fire cartridge contains basically the same components as the center-fire, with one major difference. The rim-fire does not have a primer located in the center of the cartridge as does the center-fire.

As the name implies, the rim-fire's primer is located internally around the rim of the cartridge case. The handgun's firing pin strikes the outer rim of the rim fire's cartridge, thus beginning the cartridge firing sequence.

As described in "Chapter 10, Handgun - Types and Parts," the caliber of a firearm determines the size of the projectile that it fires (it is a measurement of the rifling in the barrel of the handgun and indicates the size of the cartridge).

For example a .22 caliber firearm fires a cartridge that is approximately 0.22" in diameter; likewise, a .45 caliber firearm fires a cartridge that is approximately 0.45" in diameter.

This is generally the rule, however, some exceptions do occur, for example, the 357 Magnum and 38 Special cartridge can both be fired through a gun chambered for the .357 Magnum cartridge, and both actually have a bullet diameter of 0.357".

Parts of a Cartridge

A cartridge, often referred to as a round, consists of four following components.

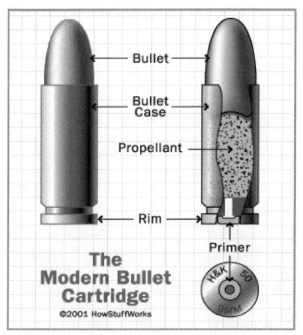

Bullet

Bullet Case

Propellant

Rim

Primer

The Modern Bullet Cartridge
©2001 HowStuffWorks

CARTRIDGE -

The cartridge is the entire assembly that is loaded into a firearm. It consists of a case, a primer, powder charge, and a bullet. The <u>case</u> is a metal cylinder closed on one end. The case is commonly made of brass and houses all other components of the cartridge.

The <u>primer</u> is an impact-sensitive device made of a chemical compound, and is located in the center of the closed end of the cartridge. Hence, the term center-fire cartridge is derived.

The <u>propellant</u> (gun powder) is a chemical compound internally contained within the cartridge. After the handgun's firing pin strikes the primer, the powder charge by means of a combustion process develops internal gases, and causing the projectile to be propelled.

(1) The <u>bullet</u> is the projectile which expels from the cartridge. The term "bullet" is frequently misused by persons incorrectly referring to the cartridge as a whole. (Diagram - item 1)

How the Cartridge actually fires a bullet . . .

In a revolver, as the shooter pulls the trigger, the hammer retracts and releases, activating the handgun's firing pin striking the cartridge's primer with sufficient force to ignite the primer, provided that a live round is in the handgun's cylinder. This action immediately ignites the cartridge's primer, the flame from the primer then ignites the powder charge.

The sudden and intense burning of the powder charge instantly produces a high volume of expanding gasses, and results in the bullet being discharged from the cartridge through the handgun's barrel to the intended target at a high rate of speed.

To ensure that your ammunition will function as it is intended, there are a few precautions which you should follow. Always store your ammunition in a cool, dry area, and do not expose it to water, solvents or other chemicals. The storage area should be climate controlled to prevent fluctuation in temperature or humidity.

Ammunition that is not properly stored or cared for may malfunction in the following way. You have fully loaded your handgun with live ammunition, and have determined that you have a safe target. You gently squeeze the handgun's trigger, CLICK, that's all you get. Instead of the explosive sound of a round firing, you only heard the sound of the handgun's action and the firing pin striking the cartridges primer.

You have just experienced a **misfire**. It is the result of a defective or otherwise damaged cartridge, and is the failure of the cartridge to fire after the primer has been struck by the handgun's firing pin.

Even though the misfire appears to be harmless, the following action must be taken.

Keep your handgun pointed in a safe direction.
Do not open the handgun's action to remove the unfired cartridge for at least 30 seconds!

After 30 seconds, open the handgun's action, remove the defective cartridge and safely dispose of it.

This safety procedure is necessary to prevent any injury to yourself or others around you should a hang fire develop.

A **hang fire** is the result of a cartridge's misfire and is a perceptible delay in the firing of a cartridge after the primer has been struck by the handgun's firing pin.

If this situation was an actual hang fire, and you had immediately opened the handgun's action after the failure of the cartridge to fire, the cartridge would have blown-up in your face or hands. Always use caution!

A **squib load** is the result of a defective or otherwise damaged cartridge, and is a failure of the cartridge to develop normal pressure or velocity for the discharging of the bullet or projectile, after the primer has been struck by the handgun's firing pin.

When firing your handgun, if a shot feels weak or the sound level of a cartridge is considerably less than normal, check for a "squib" load. A squib load is generally caused by a cartridge that was loaded without any powder, not enough powder, or the powder has been contaminated.

In some instances, the force from the primer being activated will generate enough power to expel the bullet from the case, but not enough to force it out of the barrel. Now you have a real problem that you must deal with.

If the bullet from the squib load has lodged in the handgun's barrel and you fire another shot, chances are, when the bullet contacts the lodged bullet, the barrel will rupture. This can be a dangerous situation and will cause irreparable damages to your handgun.

Always be sure of the safe operating condition of your handgun. If something doesn't sound right, check it out. If the recoil doesn't feel right, check it out. It only takes a few seconds to know for sure. Inspect and be absolutely sure that the barrel is clear of any obstructions.

Results of a SQUIB LOAD in a Semi-Automatic

A .22 CALIBER IS GOOD FOR PRACTICING . . .

Many professional handgun trainers recommend .22 caliber handguns for beginners. A .22-caliber handgun is inexpensive to purchase, and the cost of ammunition is considerably less than that of center fire ammunition. While firing, they make relatively little noise, they are extremely accurate, and have light recoil.

Although, a .22 caliber handgun is an ideal practice gun, it is not powerful enough to be used as a reliable self-defense weapon; it does not have enough stopping power.

SAFETY TIP: When buying ammunition for any firearm, carefully examine the box. Loading the wrong ammunition in your weapon is a good way to turn a good day really a bad, real fast. The ammo might load, it may even feel right, but if it is not specifically manufactured for your handgun, don't try it. The correct size ammunition is normally stamped on the side of handgun barrels.

SAFETY TIP: Your life or the life of a loved-one could be at stake, therefore, it is a good idea to know for sure that your handgun will fire the ammunition properly. It is good practice to actually test the particular type and/or brand of ammunition which you intend to use for self-defense.

SAFETY TIP: Your ammunition should be stored in a separate location from that of your handgun.

SAFETY TIP: Your ammunition should be safely secured so it is not accessible to children or unauthorized persons.

SAFETY TIP: Your ammunition should not be present when you are cleaning your firearm.

SAFETY TIP: Be certain that the ammunition is the proper ammo for your gun. The proper size or caliber ammunition for your handgun will be engraved on the handgun's barrel. Many calibers sound similar but are significantly different. Always use caution!

SAFETY TIP: When firing a handgun if a cartridge fails to fire, immediately point the weapon in a safe direction, and as a precaution in the event of a hang fire, wait at least 30 seconds, open the action and remove the cartridge.

NOW AVAILABLE FROM SHOOTERSZONE!

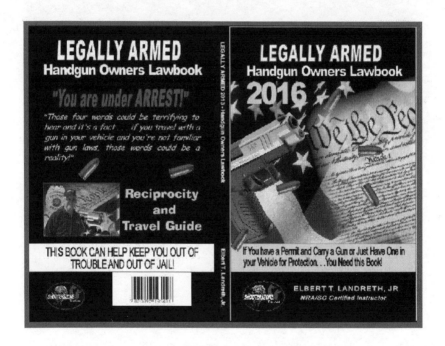

www.shooterszone.com

Chapter 12

SHOOTING FUNDAMENTALS

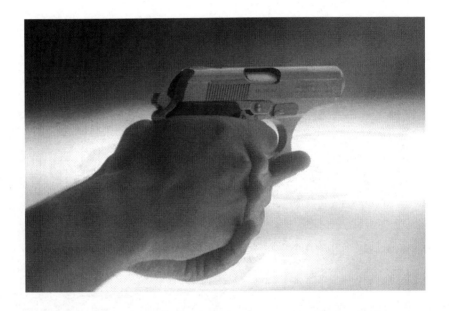

If you intend on providing yourself a reasonable amount of protection by carrying a concealed weapon, you must attain an adequate level of firearm proficiency, and that is acquired thru practice.

As the old saying goes, <u>practice makes perfect</u>. If you intend on providing yourself a reasonable amount of protection by carrying a concealed weapon, you must attain an adequate level of firearm proficiency, and that is acquired thru practice. Plan on practice sessions and be consistent.

Make your practice sessions count, try and learn something each and every time you squeeze your handgun's trigger.

Some shooters waste an unreasonable amount of time and money blasting away at a target, making no attempt to determine why they cannot shoot a tight pattern. Each shot fired should be directed to a specific spot on the target. Repetition is the name of the game. As your ability to hit a good target reliably increases, so will the speed in which you can accurately do so.

There are six basic fundamental shooting skills that must be considered and somewhat conquered before any shooter can effectively become an accomplished shooter. Those required skills are Sight Alignment, Stance (Position), Grip, Breath Control, Trigger Squeeze, and Follow-Thru, this chapter we will cover each skill thoroughly. In addition to these fundamental skills, the shooter must consider two equally important factors which play a major role in mastering shoot-

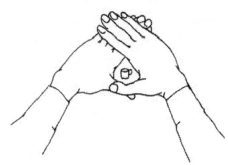

ing fundamentals; they are, determining your dominant eye, and your correct shooting hand.

Determining your Dominant Eye

The first step in preparing to be a good shooter is to determine which eye is the shooter's dominant eye. This eye the shooter will use for aiming of his or her weap-

on. The dominant eye is the stronger eye and does most of the work. A shooter should always aim with the dominant eye.

To determine your dominant eye, extend both hands to arms length. Lay one hand on the other and leave an opening in between the hands as indicated on the drawing above. Keeping both eyes open and looking through the opening (" O ") of the hands, focus on an object approximately 20 feet away. Slowly move the hands toward your face and eyes. As you continue to look through the opening in the hands at the target, you will naturally bring it to one. The eye where you finally end is your dominant eye.

Determining your Shooting Hand

A shooter will also have to determine which hand will be used to grip and fire a pistol. It is recommended that the shooter use the hand which is in the same side of the body as the dominant eye.

Now that the preliminaries are out of the way, let's focus on the fundamentals of becoming a good shooter.

SIGHT ALIGNMENT

Proper sight alignment is the relationship of the front and rear sights, and the target. The eye <u>must</u> be lined up with the front and rear sights and the sights positioned so that their alignment is correct. Proper alignment of the two sights means that the top of the front sight is even with the top of the rear sight.

The front sight must also be centered in the notch of the rear sight so that there is an equal amount of space on each side of the front sight.

Proper sight alignment is the key to accurate shooting. Any misalignment of the front with the rear sight introduces an angular error that will be multiplied with distance from the target. (See diagram at end of chapter)

The human eye is capable of focusing clearly on only one object at a time; therefore, the dominant eye cannot focus on the rear sight, the front sight and the target at the same time. You should focus on the front sight so that it appears clear and sharp.

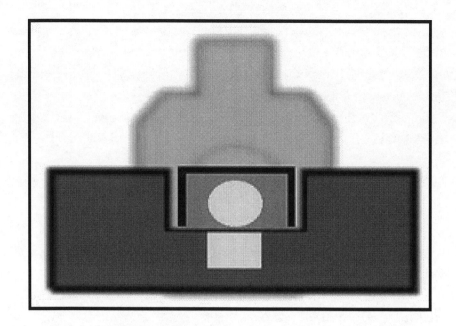

CORRECT SIGHT PICTURE

When the eye is properly focused, the front sight should appear sharp and clear, the rear sight should appear less focused, and the target will appear blurred, but visible. A correct **sight picture** is obtained by achieving proper sight alignment and then putting the aligned sights into their proper relationship with the target.

The two most important shooting fundamentals are sight-alignment and trigger-squeeze. When shooting, they should be done simultaneously while maintaining a minimum of movement.

TRIGGER SQUEEZE

Trigger squeeze is defined as the technique in which a shooter applies pressure to the trigger while firing a firearm. The finger should only be placed on the trigger immediately prior to firing a weapon. If and when the shooter is ready to actually fire a weapon, the index finger should be placed on the trigger about midway between the first joint and the tip of the finger.

The shooter should always pull the trigger straight to the rear in a smooth and continuous motion, while being careful not to disturb the sight alignment. It is practically impossible for any shooter to hold his handgun absolutely motionless, maintaining a perfect sight picture while in a firing position, this motion is called **ARC OF MOVEMENT**.

Trigger squeeze and sight alignment should be done simultaneously while maintaining a minimum arc of movement.

A shooter with good trigger control keeps his or her trigger finger independent of his or her grip. The strength of the grip should be done with your weak hand, thereby allowing the index finger of the strong hand to precisely squeeze the trigger with ease, with minimum muscular influence from the gripping fingers and thumb.

SNAP CAP

A good way to become proficient in trigger control is practice, practice, practice, and the best way is by using spring loaded snap-caps (dummy rounds). Snap-caps allow safe dry firing of your handgun without the damage that can result by firing on an empty chamber. Snap-caps contain no primer or powder charge.

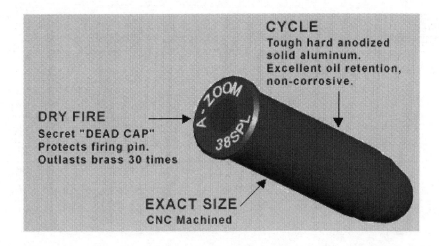

They are made of tough, easily recognizable red plastic with a solid brass base for longevity. Snap-caps are available in popular caliber sizes and made to factory ammo specs, and they can be a real asset in mastering shooting fundamentals. They are commercially available, costing less than $10.00 for a pack of 8, and they will last indefinitely.

POSITION/STANCE

A proper stance, also referred to as body position, is essential not only in shooting a good target, but in self-defense. The shooter should be standing relaxed, natural and comfortable. Many shooters feel more stable with their strong side foot back 6 to 8 inches from the other, and their body positioned in a slight boxing type of stance.

You must determine which shooting stance feels most comfortable for you, the one-handed standing position, the two-handed standing position, the weaver stance or so on. You should practice with your unloaded handgun and determine which stance feels more natural and achievable. Through repetition, you will be able to be consistent in assuming the desired position without very much conscious effort each and every time you draw your weapon.

The strong arm should be extended, but not completely rigid or locked at the elbow. The head and shoulders should remain erect and motionless. The support arm should be slightly bent at the elbow with a slight retracting effect. Try to assume the same position every time. A variety of shooting positions can be effectively used when firing a weapon, with a little time and some patience you will quickly determine which is best suited for you.

FIRING GRIP

While keeping your handgun pointed in a safe direction and your finger off the trigger, use your weak hand (non-shooting hand) to safely place the handgun in the grip of the shooting hand. Carefully fit the webbed area of the hand, where the inside of the thumb meets the inside of the index finger as high-up on the back strap of the handgun as possible, and align the handguns' frame with the wrist and forearm. Now grip the handgun with the thumb and the lower three fingers of the hand. You should have a secure, but comfortable grasp of the handgun and the index finger should be pointing parallel with the handgun.

Keep your finger off of the trigger until you are ready to fire. The thumb should be relaxed in its position along the side of the frame at a level slightly above the index finger.

Move the weak hand forward of the center of the stomach, the fingers extended and together, the palm held vertical. The palm of the hand should be held 8 to 10 inches out from the stomach. As the firing position is assumed, the weak hand should be positioned so to join and support the strong hand, as the shooter uses caution to keep the weak hand and finger's free from any movement of the handgun's action and muzzle.

The position of the weak hand must be in line, and freely movable as the handgun is pushed to full arms length toward the target for firing. Grip the handgun and hold it firmly, but comfortably. Do not clench the grips of the handgun to a degree so to cause the hand to tremble from over exertion.

Consistency plays an important role in learning how to properly grip a handgun. The shooter's grip of the handgun should be the same every time the handgun is held.

BREATH CONTROL

You should take a moderately deep breath, and then exhale enough air to be comfortable. He or she should briefly hold his or her breath before and during each shot, this minimizes body movement. The shooter should not experience any breathing difficulties during this short period of time. If the shooter is engaged in target or competition shooting, it is not necessary for the shooter to hold his breath for an extended amount of time; normal breathing should be done between shots.

FOLLOW-THRU

Follow-through is the process in which the shooter continues to apply shooting fundamentals from the preparation to fire, to the actual firing. A correct follow-through will help the shooter eliminate any unnecessary movement that might otherwise occur prior to the firing of the shot.

What this all means is quite simple, you assume the shooting stance which you feel most confident, your sights are then properly aligned on the target as previously explained; you take a breath, gently exhale until you are comfortable and hold, then in a smooth and continuous manner, you squeeze the trigger.

The follow-through is the continuing to hold as if you were in state of suspended animation. You are holding your shooting stance, your breath is still held, and your sights remain perfectly aligned with your target. Hold this position for a couple of seconds, and then relax. This technique is referred to as "follow-through." The entire process only takes a few seconds, so don't anticipate having a problem holding your breath, or holding the correct shooting position. The correct follow-through should be exercised each and every time you fire your handgun. Make it a habit.

DRAWING AND HOLSTERING THE HANDGUN

The handgun is always drawn and holstered with the safety on (in the case of a semi-automatic), the firing grip should be maintained and the trigger finger should never be inside the trigger guard. When the handgun's muzzle has cleared the holster, it should be pointing downrange in a safe direction, or toward the intended target.

When drawing and holstering the handgun, remember the following:

Keep your finger off of the trigger until you are ready to fire.

Upon drawing your handgun from the holster, it must be pointed in a safe direction.

If using a semi-auto, keep the safety on until you are ready to fire.

CONCLUSION

Finally, as with most other activities, knowledge and training are essential. If you don't know how a gun works, how can you ever begin to safely handle it or shoot it with any degree of accuracy? When you buy a new firearm, the instruction manual will explain its operation and what ammunition is compatible with your firearm.

HELPFUL HINT: The two most important shooting fundamentals are sight-alignment and trigger-squeeze.

HELPFUL HINT: When aiming a pistol, the eye can only focus on one object at a time; therefore, you should focus on the front sight so that it appears clear and sharp.

HELPFUL HINT: Proper sight alignment is having the front sight even with the top of the rear sight, and the front sight centered in the notch of the rear sight so that there is an equal amount of space on each side of the front sight.

HELPFUL HINT: Sight alignment and trigger squeeze should be done simultaneously while maintaining a minimum of movement.

HELPFUL HINT: When shooting, the trigger must be squeezed straight to the rear in a smooth and continuous manner without disturbing sight alignment.

Chapter 13

CHILDREN and GUNS

CHILD SAFETY

PROJECT CHILDSAFE SM

PUTTING A LOCK ON SAFETY IN YOUR HOME

Why should I teach my child about gun safety?

As a parent, it is your absolute, categorical, unconditional responsibility for the safety of your child, just as is the obligation to teach values and good judgment.

Statistics indicate that there is an estimated 270 million guns held by civilians in the United States, which means that the rate of private gun ownership in the US is 88.8 firearms per 100 people. Even if you do not own a gun at this particular time, odds are, you know several people that do. Your child could come in contact with a gun at your neighbor's home, or even while playing with his or her friends.

When should I teach my child about gun safety?

There is no suggested age, only you know the intelligence level of your child, therefore, you have the duty and responsibility in making that determination. A good indication as to the proper timing is when your child starts playing "cop and robbers" and "cowboy and Indians," or he or she begins to ask questions relating to the subject. When a child asks or shows interest, immediately and patiently respond.

If you don't know the correct answers, or just feel incapable in adequately discussing the subject, find a responsible and knowledgeable person that you trust and solicit their help.

Children are curious by nature, and the most effective way for a parent to help a child overcome the curiosity over firearms is to satisfy it. Talk with your child about firearms, explain how firearms have been used in past generations, their current day uses, and most important, answer your child's questions honestly and openly.

Demanding your child to stay away from or ordering them not to touch firearms will most assuredly lead to their investigating the mystery surrounding firearms for themselves, possibly with tragic results. When the mystery surrounding firearms have been dismissed from your child's mind, he or she will not see a firearm as an object of curiosity, and then the chance of a firearm-related accident can be avoided.

What should I tell my child about guns?

You should instruct your child that if he or she should ever find a firearm, or come in immediate contact through another child or a non-responsible person, they should not touch the firearm; they should promptly leave the area, and must immediately report the finding of the firearm or the presence of a firearm to you or another adult. Teaching your child that he or she may handle firearms only when you or another responsible adult is present is one of the most important lessons they can learn.

When other kids visit your home, it is comforting to have a child who knows to leave guns alone unless they're with a responsible adult. This knowledge can defuse a potentially disastrous situation. The National Rifle Association's "Eddie Eagle" program recommends that children are instructed, upon encountering a firearm, leave the area immediately without touching the firearm and go tell an adult.

SAFETY TIP: Your child should be educated and instructed to follow these safety guidelines should they ever find a firearm.

STOP!

DO NOT TOUCH THE GUN!

IMMEDIATELY LEAVE THE AREA!

GO TELL AN ADULT ABOUT THE GUN!

Please be a **Safe** and **Responsible** Firearms Owner.

Chapter 14

HANDGUN

Cleaning and Storage

Cleaning your handgun is a basic and essential part of firearm ownership. Regular cleaning and care of a handgun will extend its life for many years to come.

Cleaning your handgun is a basic and essential part of firearm ownership. Regular cleaning and care of a handgun will extend its life for many years to come. Your gun should be cleaned every time it is fired, after being exposed to dirt and/or moisture and periodically.

The first step in cleaning your handgun is to purchase a cleaning kit. There are numerous suppliers of quality gun cleaning kits, such as Remington Brite-Bore™, Kleen Bore, and Hoppe's. These are available at sporting goods stores, hardware stores and other stores such as Wal-Mart and K-Mart. Cleaning kits are available for specific caliber firearms, and are specially designed for certain types of firearms, such as rifles, pistols and shotguns.

Some manufacturers offer Universal Cleaning kits, these kits are designed for individuals who may own various types, makes and models and can be used on almost any type of modern firearm. Standard items contained in the kit are cleaning rods, cleaning solvent, oil, cleaning patches, and "end rod accessories" (used to hold the patches on the end of the rod). It's also a good idea to have an old toothbrush and a couple of clean rags handy.

Before cleaning your handgun, <u>be absolutely sure that the handgun is unloaded</u>, the action open and ammunition should not be in the immediate area where the cleaning is taking place. This is unquestionably the most important step in cleaning your handgun!

To begin the task of clearing your handgun, you should choose a work area which is well-ventilated. You will need a flat work surface on which to breakdown the handgun, for example, a workbench, desk, or tabletop. Spread a cloth over the area of the work surface in order to protect it and your handgun. Conveniently lay out your cleaning equipment and your handgun on the cloth.

Cleaning a Revolver

It is not necessary to disassemble any part of the revolver for the task of cleaning. Most modern revolvers require minimal cleaning to keep them free of rust and build-up, but will take some time to remove any lead, powder and metal fouling.

Inspect your handgun as you clean and check it for worn parts, cracks and other indications of excessive wear.

From your gun cleaning kit, gather the aluminum rod and the round brass brush for the caliber handgun you are cleaning. Attach the brush to the rod.

Now, saturate the brush with the bore cleaning solvent and insert it into the barrel of the handgun. Work the brush back and forth 6 - 8 times to free any hardened residue. Repeat as necessary.

Unscrew the brush from the cleaning rod and attach the patch holder. Dip the patch into the cleaning solvent and insert it into the barrel. Repeat these steps using clean patches until there are no signs of residues on the patches.

Attach a clean, dry patch to the cleaning rod and run it into the barrel once more to remove any remaining residue or cleaning solvent. For an exceptionally dirty barrel, insert a solvent absorbed patch through the barrel and allow the solvent to saturate for several minutes. It will help to loosen any fouling.

Attach another clean patch to the cleaning rod and place 3 -4 drop of gun barrel lubricant on the patch and run it down the barrel. This process will leave a light coat of the lubricant in the barrel, as a rust preventive. Clean and lubricate the handgun's cylinder chambers in the same manner.

To clean the handgun's action, gather the double-ended nylon brush or the old tooth brush, and saturate it with the cleaning solvent. Remove any powder residue or debris from around the action. If necessary, use a De-Greaser, such as Kleen-Bore's "Gunk-Out™," to remove loosened metal fouling and wipe clean with a clean cloth.

Finally, apply a very small amount of oil to all moving parts of the handgun. When this is completed, lightly coat the handgun's surfaces with a quality lubricate. This will help prevent rust and will extend the life of the handgun. Be careful not to over lubricate the handgun's action, this may cause the area to become tacky, allowing a buildup of dust and debris.

When you have completed the internal cleaning of the revolver, you should take a silicone gun and reel cloth, or other soft-clean cloth and very lightly coat any area of the handgun that has not been lubricated, especially, areas which have come in contact with your bare hands. This will remove any handling marks, restore the handgun's luster, and provide additional rust protection. Your handgun is now ready to be safely stored until its next use. Store your handgun in a locked container located in a cool, dry place. It is also recommended to store your handgun unloaded and separate from ammunition (unless it is used for personal protection).

Cleaning the Semi-Automatic

A semi-automatic handgun can be cleaned in a similar manner after it has been field-stripped. You should refer to your handgun owner's manual for detailed cleaning lubrication instructions. As a general rule, you should disassemble the handgun only to a point needed for you to adequately reach the areas where powder and fouling have accumulated.

Proper Handgun Storage

If the handgun is to be stored for an extended period of time, extreme care should be taken with the metal surfaces of the handgun, in order to protect them from corrosion. Do not allow handguns to come in contact with, or be stored in the close proximity of materials that attract moisture or possess a high level of acidity, or in environments with great variation of temperature or humidity.

It is just as important to securely store your handgun when it is not in use as it is to properly handle it when it is. Proper storage practices help prevent firearm accidents.

All guns that are not used for your immediate personal protection should be <u>stored unloaded, separated from ammunition</u> and in a <u>secured place that is not accessible to children and unauthorized users.</u>

Safes, lock boxes and trigger locks are effective means of securing firearms from unauthorized persons. Installing a trigger lock and storing guns in a locked cabinet will help preclude unauthorized access. Keep the keys/combination away from children. If a critical part of the gun is removed and stored separately, it is more secure.

Individuals with several firearms should seriously consider a gun safe. Several manufacturers offer models with combination locks, interlocking bolts, and optional fireproofing. Most all are designed to adequately store a combination of rifles, shotguns and handguns. Safes generally stop amateur burglars, but not professional burglars.

NOW AVAILABE FROM SHOOTERSZONE!

CCW Reciprocity and Travel Guide
www.shooterszone.com

Chapter 15

Self-Defense

The important thing to always consider in preparing for self-defense is prevention itself. It is better to avoid an attack, than find yourself in a real life shootout.

While in any public area, you should always be aware of your surroundings. *Is someone watching or following you?* Trust your instincts, if something doesn't look or feel right, you should assume that it isn't and act according. Remove yourself from the situation, immediately flee the area.

In every confrontation there is always someone a little bigger, a little faster, a little stronger, and sometimes a little luckier than the other. Chances are that you will not have the opportunity to pick-out the aggressor of your choice prior to an altercation; you will not have the luxury to pick an adversary which you know to be weaker, smaller or even less qualified than you. For that reason, you must always be prepared to handle any situation; you should become so committed to the practice of prevention that it will become second nature.

One good act of prevention is to live by an old wise tale, *"there is safety in numbers."* Walk with a friend, or seek out folks that may be heading in the same direction as you, however, you should be selective in choosing the group. When you're walking with someone else, the odds of you being attacked are greatly reduced. The old saying stands true today, *there is strength in numbers.*

If you feel that someone is following, don't go home go to an area where there are a lot of people, the more the better. Pull up to a Fire Department, Police Department, even drive down a main street of your city. If you feel an immediate threat, blow your car's horn, flash your lights; do anything within reason that will draw attention.

Walk in well-lit areas and stay away from places that you are not familiar with. If you must go to an area which you are unfamiliar with, don't go alone. In unfamiliar areas, be cautious of doorways, they can suddenly fly open and you may find yourself unwillingly being pulled by an assailant though the doorway before you know it!

Criminals sense the survival attitude and self-confidence which are displayed by persons who are well prepared, and generally direct their actions toward the weaker and less prepared as their targets. Most criminal aggressors will not risk confronting a person that is well trained in self-defense, they realize the risk of serious injury or lose of their own life could be a real threat.

The laws of nature dictate that the more prepared a person is to take the life of his aggressor in a self-defense situation, the likelihood of having to do so is greatly reduced.

Generally, you have to rely on yourself to free yourself from difficult or dangerous situations. If you find yourself in a developing confrontation, try to talk your way out of it first! That's the best technique, as expressed in an earlier chapter, *wounded feelings heal, dead bodies do not.*

However, be cautious; don't subconsciously send out signals to the aggressor that you might be weak or unprepared, just because you choose to avoid a possible deadly confrontation.

SELF-DEFENSE IS A MORAL AND LEGAL ISSUE.

Always stay ready to stand your ground and be prepared to act as the situation demands. You have the right to protect and defend yourself and your family. Anytime you have to draw your weapon in self-defense, you are committing yourself to a deadly combat.

The absolute objective of self-defense is that you inflict an injury to your adversary serious enough that it would cause him to cease the attack immediately. Just as you must be willing to take risk in defending yourself or your loved ones from a criminal attack, you must also have a mind set, that you will be willing and able to inflict serious bodily harm and even death on an attacker who has picked you to be his victim.

The laws of nature dictate that the more prepared a person is to take the life of his aggressor in a self-defense situation, the likelihood of having to do so is greatly diminished. As previously stated, criminals sense the survival instinct displayed by well-prepared persons, and most always will direct their actions and aggressions to the less prepared victims.

SAFETY TIP: Learn to remain as calm as possible, be fully alert, think clearly and you can survive an attack!

SAFETY TIP: Most muggers and attackers are cowards and almost always choose their victims who appear unsuspecting and unprepared. Don't be an "easy mark" to an aggressor, always be prepared.

SAFETY TIP: If someone asks you for directions, keep your distance and look around for their accomplice in crime.

SAFETY TIP: Unless you are absolutely positive that the area you are in is secure, wearing a headphone with your CD or tape player can create a tremendous safety risk. You cannot be fully alert to the surroundings and any looming threat.

SAFETY TIP: Keep your vehicle's gas tank filled with a sufficient amount of gas. Do not take the chance of running-out and being stranded on the side of a secluded road.

SAFETY TIP: Keep the doors locked and the windows up when you're in your car.

SAFETY TIP: Be extremely cautious about parking next to vans on the "sliding door side." You can easily be dragged inside and assaulted.

Chapter 16

PERMIT RECIPROCITY

Concealed Carry in other States

While traveling, do not make the mistake that so many others have made, and that is to assume that your states firearm and concealed carry laws apply to that of another state. That premise could be followed by your arrest for a criminal offense and a big fine, or even worse, you may find yourself in jail for months, or even years.

It is important that you understand when you are traveling in or through another state; you are subject to the laws of that state.

State firearm laws often appear somewhat similar, but more often than not, they are considerably different and their meaning contradictory to your understanding, and unless you're cautious, you could find yourself involved in an exhaustive legal battle. Even with a copy of the laws of the state in which you are traveling, the legal rhetoric contained therein can be extremely complex and difficult for the layman to understand, and *a misunderstood interpretation of the law is no legal defense in a court of law*.

It is generally presumed by the courts that every adult citizen knows the law and is held responsible for that knowledge, yet the fact is, the majority of people know absolutely nothing about the criminal laws of their own township, their county or their state, much less that of another state.

In years past when our communities were smaller in stature and its citizens were not so overwhelmed with as many laws, one could assume that the average person would be familiar with the laws, however, due to the complexity of our modern day legal system, that is no longer likely. The traveler transporting a handgun solely for self-defense must be concerned with state and federal firearm laws, and in many cases, with city and/or county ordinances. One important fact to remember is that *knowledge of the law is essential in order to avoid violating it.*

The laws providing the concealed-carry of firearms by law-abiding citizens have proven to be effective and the issuing states have expressed their satisfaction with the overall results of their states concealed-carry provisions.

Even with the vast number of permits issued by these states, records indicate that the number of persons actually charged with violation of their states criminal statues by permit holders have been very minimal.

Nevertheless, an overwhelming number of these same *legally armed* individuals who have proven to be decent, law-abiding citizens are being caught-up in unfortunate situations, which more often than not turn into serious legal problems and jeopardize the individual's freedom.

As stated earlier, <u>firearm laws differ from state-to-state and routinely places the traveler in a position where he or she unknowingly violates state firearm laws</u>. No matter how innocent the traveler may be, if a violation of the law is established by a peace officer, the traveler may, and probably will be cited for the firearm violation, and frequently, the situation results in the traveler being arrested and taken into police custody.

Before all is said and done, he or she may be convicted by the courts and subject to a hefty fine or a jail sentence, or both. This situation can be a reality to the concealed weapon permit holder and the non-permit holder alike.

Although many states recognize a concealed carry permit issued by South Carolina, it is extremely important that you know exactly which states will recognize your permit before carrying a firearm in that state.

The following states have formal concealed carry reciprocal agreements with South Carolina, or the laws of the states are such that they will honor concealed carry permit issued by South Carolina.

Alabama, Alaska, Arizona, Arkansas, Florida*, Idaho, Indiana, Iowa, Kansas, Kentucky, Louisiana, Michigan*, Minnesota, Missouri, Mississippi, Montana, Nebraska, Nevada, North Carolina, North Dakota, Ohio, Oklahoma, Tennessee, Texas, Utah, Vermont, Virginia, West Virginia, and Wyoming

* This state will <u>only</u> recognize South Carolina Concealed Weapon Permits issued to residents of South Carolina.

Chapter 17

Frequently asked questions about Concealed Weapon Permits and the "Law Abiding Citizens Self-defense Act Of 1996".

What is South Carolina's constitutional provision guaranteeing a citizen's gun rights?

> *"A well-regulated militia being necessary to the security of a free State, the right of the people to keep and bear arms shall not be infringed." Article 1, Section 20.*

Q: Am I required by the State of South Carolina to have a Concealed Weapon Permit in order to carry a handgun on or about my person?

Yes! South Carolina Code states that it is unlawful for anyone to carry about the person any pistol, whether concealed or not, except persons who are granted a permit under provision of law by the State Law Enforcement Division to carry a pistol about his person, under conditions set forth in the permit. *{South Carolina Code - Section 16-23-20}*

Q: Are there any exceptions provided by law regarding carrying a handgun?

Yes! According to South Carolina Code of Law *{South Carolina Code - Section 16-23-20}*, the following individuals are exempt;

(1) Regular, salaried law enforcement officers and reserve police officers of a municipality or county of the State, uncompensated Governor's constables, law enforcement officers of the federal government or other states when they are carrying out official duties while in this State, deputy enforcement officers of the Natural Resources Enforcement Division of the Department of Natural Resources, and retired commissioned law enforcement officers employed as private detectives or private investigators.

(2) Members of the Armed Forces of the United States or of the National Guard, organized reserves, or the State Militia when on duty.

(3) Members of organizations authorized by law to purchase or receive firearms from the United States or this State, or regularly enrolled members of clubs organized for the purpose of target shooting or collecting modern and antique firearms while these members are at or going to or from their places of target practice or their shows and exhibits.

(4) Licensed hunters or fishermen while engaged in hunting or fishing or going to or from their places of hunting or fishing.

(5) Any person regularly engaged in the business of manufacturing, repairing, repossession, or dealing in firearms, or the agent or representative of this person while possessing, using, or carrying a pistol in the usual or ordinary course of the business.

(6) Guards engaged in protection of property of the United States or any agency thereof.

(7) Any authorized military or civil organizations while parading or the members thereof when going to and from the places of meeting of their respective organizations.

(8) Any person in his home, or upon his real property, or fixed place of business.

(9) Any person in a vehicle where the pistol is secured in a closed glove compartment, closed console, or closed trunk.

(10) Any person carrying a pistol unloaded and in a secure wrapper from the place of purchase to his home or a fixed place of business or while in the process of the changing or moving of one's residence or the changing or moving of his fixed place of business.

(11) Any prison guard while engaged in his official duties.

(12) Any person who is granted a permit under provision of law by the State Law Enforcement Division to carry a pistol about his person, under conditions set forth in the permit. Persons authorized to carry weapons pursuant to items (6) and (12) of this section may exercise this privilege only after acquiring a permit from the State Law Enforcement Division as provided for in Article 4 of Chapter 31 of Title 23.

Q: Does the State of South Carolina issue *non-resident* Concealed Weapon Permits?

SLED will issue a non-resident permit to people that own real property in South Carolina, yet reside in another state.

Q: Must I have my Concealed Weapon Permit in my *possession* when I'm carrying a concealed weapon?

A permit holder must have his permit identification card in his possession whenever he carries a concealable weapon. *{South Carolina Code - Section 23-31-215 (K)}*

Q: Are there certain *places in this state that I am prohibited* by law from carrying a concealed weapon?

{South Carolina Code - Section 23-31-215} A permit issued pursuant to this section does not authorize a permit holder to carry a concealable weapon into a:

(1) police, sheriff, or highway patrol station or any other law enforcement office or facility;

(2) detention facility, prison, or jail or any other correctional facility or office;

(3) courthouse or courtroom;

(4) polling place on election days;

(5) office of or the business meeting of the governing body of a county, public school district, municipality, or special purpose district;

(6) school or college athletic event not related to firearms;

(7) day care facility or pre-school facility;

(8) place where the carrying of firearms is prohibited by federal law;

(9) church or other established religious sanctuary unless express permission is given by the appropriate church official or governing body; or

(10) hospital, medical clinic, doctor's office, or any other facility where medical services or procedures are performed unless expressly authorized by the employer. *{South Carolina Code - Section 23-31-215}*

A person who willfully violates a provision of this subsection is guilty of a misdemeanor and, upon conviction, must be fined not less than one thousand dollars or imprisoned not more than one year, or both, at the discretion of the court and have his permit revoked for five years. *{South Carolina Code - Section 23-31-215}*

Right to allow or permit concealed weapons upon premises; signs. *{South Carolina Code - Section 23-31-215}*

Nothing contained in this article shall in any way be construed to limit, diminish, or otherwise infringe upon:

(1) the right of a public or private employer to prohibit a person who is licensed under this article from carrying a concealable weapon upon the premises of the business or work place or while using any machinery, vehicle, or equipment owned or operated by the business;

(2) the right of a private property owner or person in legal possession or control to allow or prohibit the carrying of a concealable weapon upon his premises.

The posting by the employer, owner, or person in legal possession or control of a sign stating *"No Concealable Weapons Allowed"* shall constitute notice to a person holding a permit issued pursuant to this article that the employer, owner, or person in legal possession or control requests that concealable weapons not be brought upon the premises or into the work place.

A person who brings a concealable weapon onto the premises or work place in violation of the provisions of this paragraph may be charged with a violation of Section 16-11-620. In addition to the penalties provided in Section 16-11-620, a person convicted of a second or subsequent violation of the provisions of this paragraph must have his permit revoked for a period of one year. The prohibition contained in this section does not apply to persons specified in Section 16-23-20, item (1).

SECTION 23-31-225. Carrying concealed weapons into residences or dwellings.

No person who holds a permit issued pursuant to Article 4, Chapter 31, Title 23 may carry a concealable weapon into the residence or dwelling place of another person without the express permission of the owner or person in legal control or possession, as appropriate. A person who violates this provision is guilty of a misdemeanor and, upon conviction, must be fined not less than one thousand dollars or imprisoned for not more than one year, or both, at the discretion of the court and have his permit revoked for five years. *{South Carolina Code - Section 23-31-220}*

Q: If I am being questioned by a law enforcement officer, *must I inform the officer* that I am carrying a legally concealed weapon?

"A permit holder must have his permit identification card in his possession whenever he carries a concealable weapon. A permit holder must inform a law enforcement officer of the fact that he is a permit holder and present the permit identification card when an officer (1) identifies himself as a law enforcement officer and (2) requests identification or a driver's license from a permit holder." *{South Carolina Code - Section 23-31-215}*

During a contact with a peace officer, the officer may secure, or order to be secured, the weapon of the permit/license holder, throughout the duration of the contact, if the officer determines it best for security and safety reasons. The permit/license holder shall submit to the officer's request.

Q: What are the laws in this state regarding the *transporting of firearms* in a vehicle?

The South Carolina Code of Law provides any person who is not forbidden by federal and state law from owning and possessing a pistol may legally transport a pistol secured in a closed glove compartment, closed console, or closed trunk. This law applies to the resident and non-resident motorist. *{South Carolina Code - Section 16-23-20}*

Q: Is the South Carolina Concealed Weapon Permit valid in all 50 states?

NO, but you are authorized to carry a concealed weapon in the following states:

Alabama, Alaska, Arizona, Arkansas, Florida*, Idaho, Indiana, Iowa, Kansas, Kentucky, Louisiana, Michigan*, Minnesota, Missouri, Mississippi, Montana, Nebraska, Nevada, North Carolina, North Dakota, Ohio, Oklahoma, Tennessee, Texas, Utah, Vermont, Virginia, West Virginia, and Wyoming

* This state will only recognize South Carolina Concealed Weapon Permits issued to residents of South Carolina.

Q: What are the penalties in the State of South Carolina if convicted of carrying a *concealed weapon*?

Any person convicted of carrying a deadly weapon used for the infliction of personal injury concealed about his person is guilty of a misdemeanor, must forfeit to the county, or, if convicted in a municipal court, to the municipality the concealed weapon, and must be fined not less than two hundred dollars nor more than five hundred dollars or imprisoned not less than thirty days nor more than ninety days *{SC Code - Section 16-23-460}*

Q: Must I obtain a *permit to purchase* a rifle, shotgun or handgun in this state?

Rifle/shotgun? No   Handgun? No

Q: Must I *register* my rifle, shotgun or handgun in this state?

Rifle/shotgun? <u>No</u>   Handgun? <u>No</u>

Q: Am I *required to be licensed* to own a firearm in this state?

Rifle/shotgun? <u>No</u>   Handgun? <u>No</u>

Q: Is there a *waiting period* to purchase a firearm in this state?

Rifle/shotgun? <u>No</u>   Handgun? <u>No</u>

Q: What *age requirements* apply for handgun ownership in this state?

No person shall deliver a pistol to any person under the age of 18. *{South Carolina Code Section 16-23-30}*

Q: Do the laws of this state mandate *Safe Firearm Storage* or (CAP) *Child Access Protection*?

At the time of this writing, South Carolina state law does not have mandatory gun storage requirements.

Q: If I lose or misplace my Concealed Weapon Permit how do I get another one?

SLED shall issue a replacement for lost, stolen, damaged, or destroyed permit identification cards after the permit holder has updated all information required in the original application and the payment of a <u>five-dollar replacement fee.</u>

Any change of permanent address must be communicated in writing to SLED within ten days of the change, accompanied by the payment. SLED shall then issue a new permit with the new address.

<u>A permit holder's failure to notify SLED in accordance with this subsection constitutes a misdemeanor punishable by a twenty-five dollar fine.</u>

A Final Word . . .

The information presented in this book is the result of a great deal of study and research, and a fair amount of actual experience. The knowledge which you can gain from reading and studying this book may save your life, the life of someone you love, or keep you out of jail. Firearm safety must always be your *#1* concern anytime you own or have a firearm in your hands.

Since you have purchased this book and have taken the time to read it, chances are you have made a commitment to carry a self-defense firearm by virtue of a South Carolina Concealed Weapons Permit, and obtaining your permit will undoubtedly affect your life in numerous ways.

You have been advised repeatedly in this publication to be cautious, and to treat the privilege afforded the permit holder with respect. Only if you and other permit holders alike treat this right to carry a concealed handgun with respect, will the privileges and rights granted continue to be available for years to come.

Strapping on a handgun will certainly present the possibility that one day you might be forced to shoot and kill another human being as an act of self-defense, and that is serious business. The shooting or taking a human life is a tragic event and it will change your life in one way or another, even if you are totally justified in our actions.

Use your handgun in self-defense as a last resort, <u>only</u> when all other means have failed. BE SAFE and practice responsible gun ownership.

Best regards,

Ted Landreth

Other books available from Shooterszone
www.shooterszone.com

Made in the USA
Columbia, SC
12 December 2017